The Great Depression

Other Books in the History Firsthand Series:

HISTORY FIRSTHAND

The Great Depression

Dennis Nishi, *Book Editor*

David L. Bender, *Publisher*
Bruno Leone, *Executive Editor*
Bonnie Szumski, *Editorial Director*
Stuart B. Miller, *Managing Editor*
David M. Haugen, *Series Editor*

Greenhaven Press, Inc., San Diego, California

Every effort has been made to trace the owners of copyrighted material. The articles in this volume may have been edited for content, length, and/or reading level. The titles have been changed to enhance the editorial purpose.

Library of Congress Cataloging-in-Publication Data

The Great Depression / Dennis Nishi, book editor.
p. cm. — (History firsthand)
Includes bibliographical references (p.) and index.
ISBN 0-7377-0411-X (lib. : alk. paper) —
ISBN 0-7377-0410-1 (pbk. : alk. paper)
1. Depressions—1929—United States. I. Nishi, Dennis, 1967–
II. Series.

HB3717 1929 .N5   2001
338.5'42—dc21   00-052830

Cover photo: © Liaison International
Dover Publications, 91, 161
Library of Congress, 16, 19, 21, 35, 58, 70, 110, 125, 169, 205, 218

Printed in the USA

Contents

ernment bonuses. With no place to stay, they built an orderly encampment on the banks of the Anacostia River.

Chapter 3: Making a Buck

Chapter 4: Out on the Farms

Chapter 5: Taking It on the Road

Chapter 6: The New Deal

Foreword

In his preface to a book on the events leading to the Civil War, Stephen B. Oates, the historian and biographer of Abraham Lincoln, John Brown, and other noteworthy American historical figures, explained the difficulty of writing history in the traditional third-person voice of the biographer and historian. "The trouble, I realized, was the detached third-person voice," wrote Oates. "It seemed to wring all the life out of my characters and the antebellum era." Indeed, how can a historian, even one as prominent as Oates, compete with the eloquent voices of Daniel Webster, Abraham Lincoln, Harriet Beecher Stowe, Frederick Douglass, and Robert E. Lee?

Oates's comment notwithstanding, every student of history, professional and amateur alike, can name a score of excellent accounts written in the traditional third-person voice of the historian that bring to life an event or an era and the people who lived through it. In *Battle Cry of Freedom*, James M. McPherson vividly re-creates the American Civil War. Barbara Tuchman's *The Guns of August* captures in sharp detail the tensions in Europe that led to the outbreak of World War I. Taylor Branch's *Parting the Waters* provides a detailed and dramatic account of the American Civil Rights Movement. The study of history would be impossible without such guiding texts.

Nonetheless, Oates's comment makes a compelling point. Often the most convincing tellers of history are those who lived through the event, the eyewitnesses who recorded their firsthand experiences in autobiographies, speeches, memoirs, journals, and letters. The Greenhaven Press History Firsthand series presents history through the words of first-person narrators. Each text in this series captures a significant historical era or event—the American Civil War, the

Great Depression, the Holocaust, the Roaring Twenties, the 1960s, the Vietnam War. Readers will investigate these historical eras and events by examining primary-source documents, authored by chroniclers both famous and little known. The texts in the History Firsthand series comprise the celebrated and familiar words of the presidents, generals, and famous men and women of letters who recorded their impressions for posterity, as well as the statements of the ordinary people who struggled to understand the storm of events around them—the foot soldiers who fought the great battles and their loved ones back home, the men and women who waited on the breadlines, the college students who marched in protest.

The texts in this series are particularly suited to students beginning serious historical study. By examining these firsthand documents, novice historians can begin to form their own insights and conclusions about the historical era or event under investigation. To aid the student in that process, the texts in the History Firsthand series include introductions that provide an overview of the era or event, timelines, and bibliographies that point the serious student toward key historical works for further study.

The study of history commences with an examination of words—the testimony of witnesses who lived through an era or event and left for future generations the task of making sense of their accounts. The Greenhaven Press History Firsthand series invites the beginner historian to commence the process of historical investigation by focusing on the words of those individuals who made history by living through it and recording their experiences firsthand.

Introduction

In 1928 the Soviet Union began its first five-year economic plan, Amelia Earhart became the first woman to fly across the Atlantic, "Crazy Rhythm" and "Makin' Whoopee" were on the top of the music charts, and Herbert Clark Hoover was elected thirty-first president of the United States. Hoover overwhelmingly defeated governor of New York Alfred E. Smith in one of the biggest majorities in the Republican Party's history. The public's association of the Republican Party with economic prosperity had been a strong influence at the polls. But Hoover didn't share the country's enthusiasm for the booming stock market. Investors were driving up the prices of stocks in a frenzy of buying and selling. And everybody was buying on margin, which meant they were borrowing the money to invest. Buying on margin was risky because if a stock price dropped below a certain level and the bank or brokerage made a "margin call," the investor would be required to immediately repay the loan. Most investors didn't have the money, yet they continued to borrow billions of dollars nationwide to gamble on the stock market.

Unchecked speculation concerned President Hoover, who knew that the stock market was unstable. He met with Congress and the Federal Reserve Board and asked for a reevaluation of the banking policy and an increase in the rediscount rate to curb borrowing. He also suggested ways to shore up the system and spoke with the heads of top banks who were not only lending large amounts of money to brokerages but also gambling depositor money on the stock market themselves. His warnings, however, went unheeded. Policymakers and lenders were afraid of anything that could negatively affect the market. A year later, Hoover's worst fears were confirmed when the country was plunged into the worst economic crisis in its history.

Prices started dropping in September. Investors continued speculating, though, because they assumed that the market would rally, as it had many times in the past. Plus, the bargain prices for stocks were too enticing to resist. But the slide steadily continued, and picked up speed in October. Then on the morning of October 24, 1929, on the day that would become known as Black Thursday, panic ensued. With prices at an all-time low, everybody wanted to get out of the market. The sudden deluge of short selling (selling below cost) overwhelmed the markets. Author Matthew Josephson describes the hysteria:

> Panic convulsed the whole public of investors and speculators. The same mob that without reason had bid up all stocks to unreal values, now, as unreasoning before, was selling everything down, at any price. Moreover a great many of them converged upon the Wall Street community and its board rooms, thousands upon thousands of them, in order to see the continuing disaster with their own eyes. The whole world was selling America's stocks.[1]

The biggest bankers of the country pooled their resources and tried to stop the panic by buying large lots of stocks. Prices actually rose slightly but resumed falling again a few days later. Then on what would later be known as Black Tuesday, October 29, 1929, the market took the largest drop in its history. It was estimated that $30 billion was lost over the next few weeks.

Hoover was quick to respond to the crisis. He called the top business and labor leaders to Washington. He asked industry not to cut wages or lay off workers and asked labor not to fight for higher wages. In his book *Years of the Locust,* author Gilbert Seldes describes the agreement that was reached: "In the struggle between capital and labor, a truce was called, for the common good. In return for cheaper credit and lower income tax, industry promised to go ahead with programs of expansion. And the general sense of well-being spread so that cities and government departments were all prepared to spend nobly and well."[2] Industrialist Henry Ford took the agreement a step further and actually raised wages to $7 a day. His reasoning was that "American production has come to equal and even surpass, not our people's power to consume, but their power to purchase."[3]

But Americans remained cautious despite all of the reassuring propaganda that proclaimed that everything was all right. Money was withdrawn from banks and hoarded, and people became frugal. Frederick Lewis Allen writes that "economizing" set off a chain reaction:

> Trouble spread fast as servants were discharged, as jewelry shops and high-priced dress shops and other luxury businesses found their trade ebbing and threw off now idle employees, as worried executives decided to postpone building the extension to the factory, or to abandon this or that unprofitable department, or to cut down on production till the sales prospects were clearer.[4]

The United States had entered an economic slump known as the Great Depression.

Ten Years of Not Knowing

With production down, unemployment was the most pervasive problem of the Depression. At its peak, one in four Americans could not find work. Thousands of idle men walked the streets in every city and town looking for jobs. Ed Paulsen was an unemployed worker who saw the same scene everywhere he went: "I'd get up at five in the morning and head for the waterfront. Outside the Spreckles sugar refinery, outside the gates there would be a thousand men. You know dang well there's only three or four jobs."[5] Those that did manage to keep their jobs often worked more hours for less pay. But even hard work didn't assure job security. Businesses were failing every day. Every working man and woman in America knew they could be laid off at any time. It was an unsettling feeling that would last ten years.

Hoover believed that the industrialists would regain the lost initiative and the market would right itself. With this faith the president staunchly stood by his policy of refusing government aid directly to the people. He believed that handouts to the jobless weakened the spirit and undermined the self-reliance that made the country great. He continued to emphasize that it was the responsibility of the community and charities to support people in need, not the responsibility of the government. He even promoted citywide programs that encouraged volunteerism. Unfortunately, Hoover underestimated the severity of the crisis. Local shelters and city and state relief agencies were overwhelmed by the enormous number of people who needed assistance in paying rent or simply buying food and clothing. New York alone reported a 200 percent increase in aid in one year. Breadlines stretched around the block, and park benches were filled with idle men with nothing to do. Since there was no federal welfare, social security, or unemployment insurance, people who could not get relief locally had nowhere else to go. Those that couldn't pay rent or mortgages, lost their homes, or were evicted from their apartments ended up sleeping on the streets. Some people even committed crimes and let themselves be jailed so that they could have a place to stay and receive regular meals.

An Economic Solution

Hoover's answer to rising unemployment was the appropriation of $2.3 billion in federal public works spending. Building bridges, roads, and national parks not only created jobs but helped the country grow. Hoover Dam was one of the Hoover administration's biggest public works projects. Hoover also formed the President's Emergency Committee for Unemployment (PECU) and its successor, the President's Organization for Unemployment Relief (POUR). The main objectives of PECU and POUR were to promote the idea that things would soon get better. But the mostly volunteer agencies were not very successful because of underfunding and poor management. Hoover encouraged Congress to create the Reconstruction Finance Corporation (RFC). The RFC was a sort of government bank created to save local banks,

A breadline forms beside the Brooklyn Bridge. Hungry New Yorkers seeking food, shelter, and clothing overwhelmed city relief agencies.

businesses, insurance companies, and railroads from failing and thus taking away more jobs. But Hoover found industry leaders to be uncooperative. Loan recipients still continued to rely on tried-and-true methods of cutting costs by laying off workers and reducing wages. And banks held onto the money instead of loaning it out to people who needed it. Hoover later begrudgingly expanded the RFC's role to lend relief money to hard-pressed states. By then the problem was so widespread, the RFC could never offer enough help. Overall, the RFC did little during Hoover's term (it became a powerful agency during the New Deal, however, and was instrumental in recovery).

Hoover's Depression

Hoover's inability to ease the effects of the Depression earned him criticism from all sides. Despite his many optimistic predictions about recovery, the economy continued to slide. The press portrayed him as insensitive to the plight of the people and uncaring. The popular humorist Will

Rogers wrote, "It's almost been worth this depression to find out how little our big men know."[6] Hoover's name unjustly became associated with the Depression in many unflattering ways. Hoover flags were a nickname for turned-out empty pockets; Hoover blankets were the newspapers the homeless used to keep themselves warm; Hoover wagons were broken-down cars that were restored to use by being pulled by horses or mules. Hoovervilles were shanty towns built out of whatever crates, flattened tin cans, and auto parts that could be scrounged from junkyards and garbage cans. They housed the homeless. Hoovervilles were built under bridges and in any open plot of land. They had no electricity, water, or sanitation of any kind and posed many health risks. But city officials allowed them to stay because they knew that they were home to more than just hoboes; respectable middle-class families who had once held jobs also lived in Hoovervilles.

One of the biggest Hoovervilles of all was created on the doorstep of Washington, D.C., itself. In 1932 a group of veterans nicknamed the "Bonus Expeditionary Force" (BEF) marched to Washington to demand early payment of a post-wartime bonus that they had been promised. Tens of thousands of men and their families formed an orderly Hooverville community on the banks of the Anacostia River. Unfortunately, the Bonus Army was unsuccessful in getting paid in advance. The measure was voted down and the veterans that remained after the vote were driven out of Anacostia by bayonet point. General Douglas MacArthur was responsible for the rout, which resulted in death and injury. Hoover took full responsibility for his general's impulsive actions. Experts believe the Bonus Army incident contributed heavily to Hoover's defeat in his bid for reelection.

Millions on the Move

The Bonus Army wasn't alone on the roads back home. Millions of people from all walks of life had taken to the road looking for brighter prospects in the next town. There was little else to do but move when there were no jobs or relief available locally. And if there was nothing available in the next town, there was always the next state. If one could dodge the railway bulls (police) and get onto a boxcar without getting killed, freight trains offered an easy and mostly free way to get anywhere in the country. Frank Marquart recalls how crowded the trains could be: "Every Erie freight train was loaded with hoboes in those days. They rode in empty boxcars, on top of boxcars, in gondolas, on the running boards of oil tankers, and on flat cars."[7]

The Farming Crisis

Out in the country, the farmers of the nation were having an even more difficult time than their urban counterparts. They had been in trouble years before the stock market collapsed. During the First World War, farmers had increased production on their farms to meet the demands of the U.S. War Department and European nations. But after the war ended the farmers continued to produce the same amount despite the drop in demand. This resulted in a large surplus of goods that drove down prices. In 1920 a bushel of wheat sold for $3, but by the end of 1932 a bushel could only bring 30 cents. It often cost more to harvest crops than they could be sold for. And since many farmers had gone into debt buying additional land and new equipment, a large number of farms were lost to bank foreclosures. Many farmers were understandably angry for essentially being prosperous but losing everything. Some starving farmers took up arms to feed themselves and their families. T.H. Watkins writes about an incident that made the papers in Minnesota: "On February 25, several hundred men and women smashed the windows of a grocery and meat market in Minneapolis and grabbed bacon and ham, fruit and canned goods. When one of the store owners drew a revolver, the crowd jumped him and broke his arm."[8]

Farmers in the panhandle states of Texas, Oklahoma, New Mexico, Kansas, and Colorado had experienced a different kind of problem. Overcultivation and drought had created an environmental catastrophe that resulted in millions of tons of topsoil being blown into the air. The panhandle region became known as the dustbowl because of the violent dust storms that blew dust as far away as Chicago. The conditions were so bad that farmers just packed up their families and left their worthless plots of land without looking back. They drove west across Route 66, pursuing rumors of jobs in California. But the job market in California was as depressed as that of the rest of the country. And West Coast landowners took advantage of the sudden glut of workers by dropping wages, sometimes below the subsistence level. *The Grapes of Wrath,* by John Steinbeck, tells the story of a family from Oklahoma who migrated West and found life there to be quite different than what they had left behind. In his tragic novel, Steinbeck writes,

> The moving, questing people were migrants now. Those families which had lived on a little piece of land, who had lived and died on forty acres, had eaten or starved on the produce of forty acres, had now the whole West to rove in. And they scampered about, looking for work; and the highways were streams of people, and the ditch banks were lines of people. Behind them more were coming.[9]

Facing dustbowl conditions in the panhandle states, migrants are forced to travel as far west as California in search of work.

A New President

After three years of hardship, the American public expressed their dissatisfaction with Herbert Hoover. In 1932, they elected governor of New York Franklin Delano Roosevelt as president in a landslide victory. Roosevelt was a different kind of man than Herbert Hoover. Roosevelt came from a life of privilege in New York and was a career politician who dedicated his life to public service. Hoover was a mining engineer and a self-made man who made his fortune in business. The two presidents were both compassionate men who sought to ease suffering but practiced different philosophies of government. Whereas Hoover had tried to preserve the spirit of self-reliance and practice a hands-off approach toward business, Roosevelt believed in widely expanding the role of government in relieving economic hardship and protecting the public from business. He described his plans as the New Deal. This was a completely new approach since the government had historically practiced a more laissez-faire (let people do as they choose) policy of individual and business freedom. But after three years of overflowing unemployment offices and endless breadlines, Americans wanted the government to become more involved.

The Bank Holiday

The problem that required immediate attention was the banking crisis. Since the stock market crash, thousands of U.S. banks had failed. The entire banking system was on the verge of collapse. Before the Glass-Steagall Banking Act in 1933, there was no such thing as federal deposit insurance. When a bank failed, it took the life savings of thousands of Americans with it. This uncertainty incited panic in depositors, who rushed to their banks after the crash to pull all their money out and hoard it. But mass withdrawals were impossible to grant because banks did not keep all of their depositors' money in a vault. Each branch only kept enough money to accommodate the daily needs of the average customer. The rest of the money was invested in loans to other depositors, bonds, and outside investments. The profit was

A failed bank shuts its doors after panicked depositors withdraw their money following the stock market crash.

returned in part to depositors in the form of interest dividends. But in the early stages of economic panic, depositors didn't want dividends, they wanted their life savings returned to them. When enough depositors withdrew their money, a bank could be put out of business.

Acting on an earlier recommendation by Hoover, Roosevelt declared a four-day bank holiday, shutting banks to the fearful depositors wanting to withdraw their funds. The breather prevented more money from being withdrawn and gave Roosevelt the opportunity to calm the public. The weekend following the announcement was a tense one, wrote William Manchester, because no one could get money easily:

> Many of the newsboys peddling the extras were obliged to sell on credit. Those who did collect coins found themselves hailed by cruising merchants waving bills and pleading for change. A few storekeepers, unable to locate silver, had to close their stores; those who sought relief in Windsor, Ontario, were coldly told their checks would be "subject to collection," and under the phony holiday air there was a feeling of uneasiness about the value of what currency there was.[10]

The holiday also gave the Reconstruction Finance Corporation time to examine bank records and decide which banks were solvent. The soundest banks were allowed to reopen the following week, but the banks with financial problems were forced to reorganize under the supervision of the government. The Emergency Banking Act was drafted and passed in a special session of Congress to officially authorize these actions.

The Fireside Chats

Roosevelt went on the radio the following Sunday to explain to the American public what was being done about the banking situation. His manner was informal and friendly. He used accessible language that average citizens could understand to explain banking mechanics and let people know what they needed to do to help overcome the crisis: "You people must have faith; you must not be stampeded by rumors or guesses. Let us unite in banishing fear. We have provided the machinery to restore our financial system; and it is up to you to support and make it work."[11] This was the first time radio was used in this way by a president. The press called Roosevelt's speech a "fireside chat" and this one and future ones proved to be very effective in allaying public fears throughout the Depression. When the banks opened the following week, more people lined up to make deposits than to make withdrawals.

Immediate Action

Throughout his presidency, Hoover had fought to limit spending and keep the budget balanced. Roosevelt had no such reservations about appropriating billions of dollars toward relief programs. It was one of his primary goals upon becoming president to supply relief to as many people that needed it as soon as possible and at whatever cost. In an election speech, he had stated, "If starvation and dire need on the part of any of our citizens make necessary the appropriation of additional funds which would keep the budget out of balance, I shall not hesitate to tell the American people the truth and ask them to authorize the expenditure of that additional amount."[12] Roosevelt promised immediate and drastic action, and he wasted no time in fulfilling that promise. In what became known as the Hundred Days, a flood of new legislation was created and whipped through both legislative houses. A cooperative Congress passed almost every emergency measure Roosevelt and his advisers came up with. Some critics worried that Roosevelt wielded more power than any president was meant to have. Concerned citizens even wrote letters to their representatives questioning where the country was going.

> My Dear Senator: It seems very apparent to me that the Administration at Washington is accelerating its pace towards socialism and communism. Nearly every public statement from Washington is against the stimulation of business which would in the end create employment. Everyone is sympathetic to the cause of creating more jobs and better wages for labor; but, a program continually promoting labor troubles, higher wages, shorter hours, and less profits for business, would seem to me to be leading us fast to a condition where the Government must more and more expand its relief activities, and will lead in the end to disaster to all classes.[13]

T.H. Watkins remarks that it was merely necessity taking advantage of opportunity: "Such tender acquiescence on the part of Congress would not last forever, and the New Dealers struck swiftly and often while the legislative iron was hot."[14]

The Civilian Conservation Corps

What followed the Hundred Days was an array of experimental acts and agencies that placed a government hand into every aspect of business and the economy. The programs had long descriptive names and so became known by their initials. They were all nicknamed the alphabet agencies and were designed to offer relief and speed economic recovery. The Civilian Conservation Corps (CCC), one of the first New Deal programs, had the highest profile. Unemployment was a persistent problem throughout the Depression and an issue Roosevelt was committed to resolving. He formed the

CCC to help young unmarried men by taking them off the street and giving them jobs. They received food, clothing, shelter, and a $30-a-month wage (most of which went to the families) to work for the government. Some, for example, labored in the national forests and parks building roads and bridges and fighting fires. The program, created through the Unemployment Relief Act, placed the agency under the jurisdiction of the Departments of Labor, War, Agriculture, and the Interior. Although the CCC followed a military model of discipline, it was not a military organization. Critics argued that the program needed to be expanded since it only helped young men. Thomas Minehan wrote, "What we need is a new Child Conservation Corps. Which will have as its purpose the saving not of our forests a hundred years from today, but of our boys and girls growing into the men and women of tomorrow."[15] The CCC continued until 1943 when the Second World War required the manpower reserves of the nation.

Relief for the Farmers

The farming crisis was another problem Roosevelt quickly addressed. Prices were bottoming out, and violence was erupting all over farm country. The U.S. Communist Party and other radical labor groups were swarming all over the Midwest rallying farmers and assisting protests. Many thought a revolution might occur. Roosevelt called farm leaders to Washington to help create the Agricultural Adjustment Act (AAA). The AAA paid farmers to produce less, which would raise market prices. This involved planting fewer crops or plowing under existing crops and slaughtering pigs and cows. The money for the subsidies would be raised by charging a tax to the food processing industry, such as canneries. It was a radical idea that shocked many, including Secretary of Agriculture Henry Wallace, who grudgingly implemented the program. The AAA did raise prices slightly but had an unexpected effect on tenant farmers. Tenancy was an old institution in which farmers rented farmland and paid landowners a share of their crops. Tenant farmers had always been exploited, and many could not even eke out a marginal existence on what they earned after paying the landowner. After the AAA came into effect, many landowners used the federal money to buy modern tractors, then evicted their tenants to reclaim their rented land in hopes of expanding and modernizing their farms.

Flying the Blue Eagle

The National Industrial Recovery Act (NIRA) was signed into law in June 1933. It created the National Recovery Administration (NRA), which was a long-term economic solution for business and labor. The plan sought to establish 550 self-regulating codes and standards. Some of these new codes included the institution of a minimum wage, maximum work hours, safer working conditions, and the guarantee that workers had the right to organize and bargain collectively. Roosevelt hoped to end the conflict between owners and workers in an effort to get industry rolling again. On September 30, 1934, he addressed the nation to discuss the NRA:

> I shall not ask either employer or employees permanently to lay aside the weapons common to industrial war. But, I shall ask both groups to give a fair trial to peaceful methods of adjusting their conflicts of opinion and interest and to experiment for a reasonable time with measures suitable to civilize our industrial civilizations.[16]

The inspired New Deal program was represented by a big blue eagle and the motto "We Do Our Part." Anybody who complied with the codes could display the eagle on their flag masts or in their store windows. However, the NRA did not contribute much to economic recovery. Many businesses signed up but continued to run things the way they always had. Automaker Henry Ford refused to participate in the program at all. There were many points that couldn't be agreed on universally. Without industry-wide cooperation, the system could not work.

The second and more successful section of the NIRA

created the Public Works Administration (PWA) and the Civil Works Administration (CWA). Both programs created millions of new public works jobs such as building ports, schools, hospitals, power plants, and dams. The programs required the purchase of billions of dollars in equipment and supplies, which put money right back into the economy.

The National Industrial Recovery Act was strongly criticized for meddling in the private sector. Many didn't believe that the government should be allowed to interfere in business and impose regulations that critics thought would hinder recovery as opposed to help it. But many others in the nation felt the crisis called for drastic measures. The fact was, however, that some of the New Deal programs had overstepped the bounds of federal authority. In 1935 the NRA and its parent act the NIRA were declared unconstitutional by the Supreme Court. Yet other alphabet agencies lived on.

The Government Becomes a Patron of the Arts

The Great Depression was very well documented thanks in part to the New Deal's Works Progress Administration (WPA). The government became one of the biggest sponsors of the arts, employing 8.5 million artists during the WPA's lifetime. Actors and directors were hired to produce plays, painters painted murals for post offices and libraries, composers composed music, and writers were hired to write. From 1936 to 1940, the Federal Writers Project paid sixty-five hundred writers $20 a week to go out and interview ordinary people and get their life stories. There are more than 10,000 of these accounts archived by the Library of Congress. Many now-famous writers who might not ever have been recognized got their start with the WPA. African American writers like Richard Wright and Zora Neale Hurston wrote for the WPA. Even John Steinbeck worked briefly for the WPA by conducting a census of dogs in Monterey. The WPA was one of the longest lived New Deal agencies, and its contribution to recording part of the nation's history remains a testament to its importance and its success.

New Changes for a New Era

A thoroughly documented depression was new to Americans, but depressions themselves were not. The United States had experienced many economic downturns and periods of mass unemployment in the past. But none had ever been as severe as the Great Depression of the 1930s. This depression was different from previous depressions in many ways. It took hold of the country much faster than previous events and affected a wider number of people. The rich and the poor and all the classes in between were indiscriminately affected by what many called a national blight. Nobody was completely insulated from what was happening. The Depression was the topic of daily discussion. It was talked about on the radio and portrayed in the movies. Despite all of the widespread hardships, the country underwent a transformation socially, politically, and technologically. This is clearly shown in the many history records and oral histories of the people from the time. People faced with a crisis were forced to think a different way, and as a nation they overcame.

Hoover and Roosevelt represented more than the passing of one president to another. The New Deal programs forever changed the relationship between the individual, business, and government. Hoover had employed policy and methods that had been successful in the past. He worked within the then-limited framework of a government that had traditionally been granted limited control of people and business. But the Depression showed that something revolutionary was needed not only to relieve suffering but to promote growth in the long term.

In 1939 it was estimated that 9.2 million people were still unemployed. The country had just come off a recession (a period of low economic activity). Overall the nation was better off than it was six years before, but the New Deal had been unsuccessful in shaking the effects of the Depression. It took the threat of the Second World War to put U.S. industry back on its feet and restore full employment. After Germany had annexed Austria and invaded the Sudetenland and Poland in 1939, orders for war materials flooded into the United States from panicked European countries. Factories that had been closed for years were reopened to accommodate the orders. Every industry in the United States was alit with activity and jobs. Spending accompanied regular paychecks, driving up demand and prices. It was the same economic boom experienced before and after the First World War. But this time there were safeguards in the system that would prevent anything like the crisis of the 1930s from ever happening again.

Notes

1. Matthew Josephson, *The Money Lords*. New York: Weybright and Talley, 1972, pp. 88–89.
2. Gilbert Seldes, *The Years of the Locust: America, 1929–1932*. Boston: Little, Brown, 1933, p. 48.
3. Quoted in Seldes, *The Years of the Locust,* p. 48.
4. Frederick Lewis Allen, *Since Yesterday*. New York: Bantam Books, 1940, p. 21.
5. Quoted in Studs Terkel, *Hard Times*. New York: Pantheon Books, 1970, p. 32.
6. Quoted in Milton Meltzer, *Brother Can You Spare a Dime?* New York: Alfred A. Knopf, 1969, p. 92.
7. Frank Marquart, *An Auto Worker's Journal: The UAW from Crusade to One-Party Union*. Philadelphia: Pennsylvania State University Press, 1975, p. 42.
8. T.H. Watkins, *The Great Depression: America in the 1930s*. Boston: Little, Brown, 1993, p. 80.
9. John Steinbeck, *The Grapes of Wrath*. New York: Alfred A. Knopf, 1993, p. 362.
10. Quoted in Don Congdon, *The 30s: A Time to Remember*. New York: Simon and Schuster, 1962, p. 130.
11. Quoted in Russell D. Buhite and David W. Levy, eds., *FDR's Fireside Chats*. New York: Penguin Books, 1992, pp. 15–16.
12. Quoted in Frank Freidel, ed., *The New Deal and the American People*. Englewood Cliffs, NJ: Prentice-Hall, 1964, p. 12.
13. Quoted in Robert McElvaine, *Down and Out in the Great Depres-*

sion: Letters from the "Forgotten Man." Chapel Hill: University of North Carolina Press, 1983, p. 60.

14. Watkins, *The Great Depression*. p. 122.

15. Thomas Minehan, *Boy and Girl Tramps of America*. New York: Grosset & Dunlap, 1934, p. 134.

16. Quoted in Buhite and Levy, *FDR's Fireside Chats*, p. 60.

Chapter 1

It Started on Wall Street

Chapter Preface

B efore the stock market crash, the nation was riding on a wave of euphoria. Confidence was high and the stock market was up. Everybody seemed to be making a fortune by speculating in the stock market. Between August and September 1929, almost 1.1 billion transactions were made. A common story that circulated around the brokerages told of the shoeshine boy or waitress who had parlayed their tip money into a million. But in actuality, most people in the country did not have the extra money to invest in the market. Those few that did invest increased their buying power by borrowing money. All of this speculation and extension of credit was what destabilized the stock market.

In September 1929 the stock market took a downward trend and continued to slide through October. Then on October 29, 1929, in what would become known as Black Tuesday, the bottom fell out of the stock market. Historians considered it the worst day in the history of stock markets. There was so much panicked selling that the market fell behind on posting the most current prices. It became agonizing to watch fortunes disappear. Sixteen million shares were sold, and more were put up for sale that could not be sold for any price. By mid-November $30 billion had been lost. This was more than the United States had spent on World War I and almost twice the amount of the national debt.

The October crash did not cause the Depression. There were many factors that preceded the crash that contributed to the crisis. The farmers of the nation had never recovered from the recession of the 1920s, and overproduction had driven food prices down. However, it was the Wall Street crash that historians mark as the beginning of the most pervasive crisis in U.S. history.

The Crash

Matthew Josephson

Beginning on Monday, October 21, 1929, prices on the stock exchange began to drop. For eight days panicked sellers inundated the stock exchange in a frenzy of selling. There were so many sale orders that the ticker tape machines could not keep up with the volume. Matthew Josephson was a stockbroker in the twenties. He witnessed the crash on Wall Street firsthand. The following excerpt is taken from his biographical book, which describes the crash and the measures the big bankers employed trying to stabilize the market.

O ne is led to believe that nobody, or almost nobody, saw what was coming. The summer of 1929 was a season of euphoria in the financial world, although reports of declining factory output, automobile sales, and railway freight traffic were coming in as warning signals. The high Reserve Bank money rate was also a traditional signal for retreat.

In September the market leaders reached their peak; many blue chips [the most stable and consistently profitable stocks], undergoing corrective reaction, looked "ragged," and, with few exceptions, tended to decline gently during the first half of October. On Friday, October 18, the whole market began to go down swiftly, and declined even more sharply in the next day's half session. The same steep downward trend continued on Monday, with high-grade stocks such as General Electric and American Telephone losing five to ten points. Leading economists such as Professor Irving Fisher of Yale, and the magnates Mitchell and Raskob,

Excerpted from *The Money Lords* (New York: Weybright and Talley, 1972) by Matthew Josephson. Copyright © 1972 by Matthew Josephson. Reprinted with permission from Harold Ober Associates.

made cheerful pronouncements to the press; but an attempt to rally the market failed, and panicky selling came in strong on Wednesday, October 23. The high-priced favorites fell through veritable air pockets, with Westinghouse dropping 35, General Electric 20, and Commercial Solvents all of 70 in a single session that saw an unprecedented trading volume of six million shares. Now there were reports of many margin calls being sent by brokers to their clients.

The next day—Black Thursday—panic convulsed the whole public of investors and speculators. The same mob that without reason had bid up all stocks to unreal values, now, as unreasoning as before, was selling everything down, at any price. Moreover, a great many of them converged upon the Wall Street community and its board rooms, thousands upon thousands of them, in order to see the continuing disaster with their own eyes. The whole world was selling America's stocks.

Eyewitnesses recall the crowds of Thursday, October 24, filling the streets outside the Stock Exchange and standing on the steps of the old sub-Treasury Building, silent, expressionless, as if turned to stone. I was no passive onlooker, for I had my own small stake in that demented market. In the past year my portfolio of securities, purchased with the proceeds of a modest inheritance, had doubled in value, though I managed my account entirely on a cash basis. I had hoped to work up a little competence to allow me at least partial economic security, so that I could write as I pleased. The wished-for competence had now gone up the chimney—"where the woodbine twineth"—as the old traders used to say. I had shared for a while the hopes, even the illusions of America's middle class and now suffered their common fate.

What had triggered the "greatest stock market catastrophe of the ages," as the sober *Commercial and Financial Chronicle* described it? The gradual erosion of values in September and early October had undermined margin accounts; when brokers began to call for cash, or to "dump" pledged securities in under-margined accounts, the downward movement became an avalanche. The numerous investment trusts that had been relied on to bolster the market were then driven to make forced sales of large blocks; their blue chips fell. Some of them from 300 or 400 per share by 77 to 96 points in an afternoon, as on October 23. The next morning *there were simply no bids* at all for the equities of America's largest corporations.

Panic Sweeps the Floor

I remember on one of those days, October 23, taking the subway downtown to visit my broker's board room. It was a minute or two before 10:00 A.M. as I reached the Wall Street station. I heard—and I can still hear it—the sound of running feet, the sound of fear, as people hastened to reach posts of observation before the gong rang for the opening of trading. Hypnotized by their panic, the crowds in the board rooms stared in horror at the stockboards or the tape recording their ruin. Brokers and their clerks, who had been up all night at their paperwork, calling for margin hour-by-hour, looked drawn and haggard. Owing to the record-breaking volume of trades, which swamped all communication facilities, the tape fell two hours behind, then, by noon, four hours behind! You could see your General Electric on the tape at $180, but the floor broker's telephoned message from Broad Street said that it was really selling for $40 or $50 less! Even the clocks seemed to have gone wrong. The crowds of customers in the board rooms all reacted in different ways. Some cried out their astonishment at the unfamiliar prices they saw, or at the sweeping changes in their fortunes recorded in a few hours, or even minutes; others laughed in disbelief, or made little self-deprecating jests, such as, "It's only money," or "easy-come easy-go," But it was too stunning an affair to be laughed off; a whole great class, between two and three million American families, were being stripped of their wealth.

"They'll all come back," a broker said cheerily. I wanted to believe it, but doubts assailed me. Things seemed to have gone too wildly wrong to be righted easily. Few living men had ever seen such a panic.

As always, the bell rang at 3:00 P.M. for the close of trading, but everyone stood riveted there for two, three, or more hours longer watching the retarded tape tap out the unthinkable losses of that day. During the fortnight that followed October 24, about $34 billion in market value disappeared! The whole Wall Street citadel of wealth and power, with all its paper symbols, had collapsed in ruin.

Caught Off Guard

The newspapers covering the day's events made quite a legend of how the "Morgan bankers consortium" on Black Thursday had contained the panic by sending Richard Whitney to the Exchange to bid up leading stocks. (They did not stop the decline then.) Actually, when the market began its great downward plunge, the leading men in finance were caught off guard. J.P. Morgan was in England, Charles E. Mitchell had sailed to Germany, and E.H.H. Simmons, veteran president of the Stock Exchange, who had lately remarried in his old age, was honeymooning in Honolulu.

The big bankers in New York kept in touch with one an-

People gather outside of the New York Stock Exchange after the crash of October 24, 1929, now known as Black Thursday.

other by telephone. At noon on October 24, Albert H. Wiggin of the Chase Bank, sitting before his ticker, was heard to exclaim, "This is no bear market, it's a panic—we have got to do something." He put on his hat and headed for the Corner, out of habit, and because Thomas W. Lamont [an American banker] had called him to a lunchtime meeting. At Broad and Wall he almost collided with Mitchell, who had hurried back from Europe on receiving the dire news from home. George F. Baker, Jr., chairman of the First National Bank, was on hand, as was W.C. Potter of the Guaranty Trust, and other bigwigs; Lamont presided. An important personage among those present was George L. Harrison, the new Governor of the Federal Reserve Bank of New York, who had succeeded the late Benjamin Strong. He was a bureaucrat but he commanded the funds of the largest Reserve Bank. At this first hasty conference the bankers agreed to supply credits of up to $240 million for a syndicate that would buy leading stocks and thus try to stabilize the market. The bankers' "pool" was the same scheme that the elder Morgan had used to stem panics in past times. The press was waiting for word.

Someone urged that the Stock Exchange be closed down, as at the opening of World War I, but he was overruled. Their syndicate must begin to buy. But would it work to stop the raging panic? No one really knew if there would be enough money available to the banks to take over the tremendous amount of brokers' loans that was expected to be called (by non-bankers) the next day. But one thing they agreed upon was that they must work together to restore confidence—for confidence, that precious, elusive thing, had flown. Meanwhile the bankers preserved an icy calm; and the vivacious Lamont tried to reassure the public in a low-keyed press statement admitting that "there had been a little distress selling."

Trying to Restore Confidence

In the course of their meeting they had drawn up a list of stocks to be bought and handed it to Richard Whitney, well known to be "Morgan's broker." As vice president of the Stock Exchange, Whitney was now, in the absence of Mr. Simmons, its acting president. At 1:30 P.M. his large, well-groomed figure was seen striding swiftly across the floor of the Exchange toward Post 2. Fevered newspaper accounts described him as "running" or "charging like a bull" into the crowd trading in U.S. Steel; but running on that floor has always been forbidden. Whitney called out to the specialist broker at the "Steel" post: "I bid two hundred and five for twenty-five thousand Steel." This was quite an order, amounting to $5 million, at a price above the last sale. The market rallied, Steel steadied at 206¼. Whitney then went on to the trading posts where specialists kept book on other blue chip stocks, offering to buy large amounts in blocks of 10,000 to 25,000 shares at prices somewhat above the market. A modest rally had already begun at noon when it was reported that several leading New York bankers had been seen going into Morgan's. J.P. Morgan and Company were formerly thought to control the banking and investment world of New York and even, some believed, the machinery of the New York Stock Exchange, whose powerful governing committees were usually led by persons like Richard Whitney, wearing the "Morgan collar." The Morgans were the great insiders and their prestige was at its height. The advent of Whitney, society man and fox hunter, regularly used as the great bank's floor broker for routine buying of gilt-edged bonds, had its psychological impact; his bids lent strength to the momentary rally, so that prices for that session showed a partial recovery. Over land and sea went the word: *"Richard Whitney halts stock panic*—Morgan broker buys 25,000 Steel at 205—Heroic action rallies market." National fame touched Whitney from that moment on. Everywhere he was known as "the man who halted the market panic of 1929" and as a gentleman of sublime "courage." Actually, he had bought much less than was supposed— only two hundred shares of Steel, for example. He had done a bit of stage acting, reducing his buying as prices rose a little. The bankers were not throwing their cash away like drunken sailors, but they were anxious to conserve a war chest for future use in worse emergencies that some of them had good reason to expect.

A Brief Stay

Meanwhile there was the roar of cheers, as on a battlefield after a successful charge. Dick Whitney had become the hero of the day, and all that he did henceforth was to be as if touched with deeper meaning—the way he smiled narrowly and his merest wisecracks were noted and reported everywhere. A few months later the grateful members of the Stock Exchange elected him president in place of Simmons. At forty-two he was the youngest man ever honored with that office. Whitney embodied the grand old myth of the Morgan bank's power and leadership dating from the golden years of "Jack" Morgan's father, J. Pierpont Morgan, who acted as *the* central bank of New York before there was a Federal Reserve System, and towered over other financiers by sheer force of character and will. But that myth was soon dissolved amid scenes of universal selling, renewed after the weekend and continued in great waves for days on end.

The "hero of the day" looked his part, as if he had been selected with care out of an army of Hollywood extras. He was impeccably and formally dressed; a big man physically, over six feet tall, he carried his two hundred and ten pounds lightly, with the tread of a former Harvard athlete. His features were large, regular, and handsome in a heavy way; his hair was jet black, a little flecked with gray, and his eyes deep set under prominent downward slanting brows. If one had been able to catch up with him during those turbulent days, he might himself have explained that he was, in fact, no hero at all. What he did was only in the line of business: it was not his money but that of the bankers' syndicate he was employing, and no "courage" on his part was involved. Moreover, his grandstand play of October 24, 1929, worked for only a short time, only two days.

Whitney had served in fairly routine fashion as a Morgan functionary on the Exchange for seventeen years. He himself was a model of the old nepotistic Yankee plutocracy in the Street, where rich families, after having their sons polished at Groton School and Harvard, put them to work in stocks and bonds, Through his family, Whitney had close ties to Morgan's—his elder brother George was a partner there. He had married an heiress, lived in a Fifth Avenue town house, and as a country squire, in an estate in the fashionable suburb of Far Hills, New Jersey. Richard Whitney carried himself with the aplomb and pride befitting a representative of the old Wall Street elite. But this did not endear him to the new breed that operated without the favor of the Morgans, such as "Joe" Kennedy and Bernard E. Smith.

The Panic Resumes

There had been a lull in the storm and Whitney was able to take an early train to New Jersey on Saturday and preside over a meeting of the Essex Fox Hounds—"something I really like," he said. But on Monday torrential selling engulfed the market again; trading volume rose to sixteen million on one of the worst days that followed, when, as Whitney related, the Exchange's counting machine broke down. His own informed guess for that record-breaking volume of trade was "over twenty-three million shares, counting odd lots."

Something like insanity possesses our "free and liquid market" for securities in such seasons of high excitement: on one day men seem wildly eager to exchange their hard cash for the paper of "Radio" at 500, or "Alleghany" at 50, because they spell high profits; on another day the same speculators stampede to sell their shares at no matter what price so that they may realize their cash again.

Picking Up the Pieces

Arthur Robertson

While a growing number of businesses and banks declared bankruptcy every day, a few opportunistic individuals weathered the crash and took advantage of the panic. Arthur Robertson made his fortune by buying these bankrupt businesses for low prices and later reselling them for enormous profits. In the following interview with Studs Terkel he tells of how his good business instincts kept him from overspeculating in the market while fellow financiers couldn't seem to restrain themselves. Although the speculators lost their shirts, Robertson survived the crash and—at age twenty-four—became a multimillionaire during America's bleakest economic crisis.

In 1929, it was strictly a gambling casino with loaded dice. The few sharks taking advantage of the multitude of suckers. It was exchanging expensive dogs for expensive cats. There had been a recession in 1921. We came out of it about 1924. Then began the climb, the spurt, with no limit stakes. Frenzied finance that made [Charles] Ponzi look like an amateur. I saw shoeshine boys buying $50,000 worth of stock with $500 down. Everything was bought on hope.

Today, if you want to buy $100 worth of stock, you have to put up $80 and the broker will put up $20. In those days, you could put up $8 or $10. That was really responsible for the collapse. The slightest shake-up caused calamity because people didn't have the money required to cover the other $90 or so. There were not the controls you have today. They just sold you out: an unwilling seller to an unwilling buyer.

A cigar stock at the time was selling for $115 a share. The market collapsed. I got a call from the company president. Could I loan him $200 million? I refused, because at the time I had to protect my own fences, including those of my closest friends. His $115 stock dropped to $2 and he jumped out of the window of his Wall Street office.

There was a man who headed a company that had $17 million in cash. He was one of the leaders of his industry and controlled three or four situations that are today household words. When his stock began to drop, he began to protect it. When he came out of the second drop, the man was completely wiped out. He owed three banks a million dollars each.

The banks were in the same position he was, except that the government came to their aid and saved them. Suddenly they became holier than thou, and took over the businesses of the companies that owed them money. They discharged the experts, who had built the businesses, and put in their own men. I bought one of these companies from the banks. They sold it to me in order to stop their losses.

The worst day-to-day operators of businesses are bankers. They are great when it comes to scrutinizing a balance sheet. By training they're conservative, because they're loaning you other people's money. Consequently, they do not take the calculated risks operating businesses requires. They were losing so much money that they were tickled to get it off their backs. I recently sold it for $2 million. I bought it in 1933 for $33,000.

The Scavenger

In the early Thirties, I was known as a scavenger. I used to buy broken-down businesses that banks took over. That was one of my best eras of prosperity. The whole period was characterized by men who were legends. When you talked about $1 million, you were talking about loose change. Three or four of these men would get together, run up a stock to ridiculous prices and unload it on the unsuspecting public. The minute you heard of a man like [William] Durant or Jesse Livermore buying stock, everybody followed.

They knew it was going to go up. The only problem was to get out before they dumped it.

Durant owned General Motors twice and lost it twice . . . was worth way in excess of a billion dollars on paper, by present standards, four or five billion. He started his own automobile company, and it went under. When the Crash came, he caved in, like the rest of 'em. The last I heard of him I was told he ended up running a bowling alley. It was all on paper. Everybody in those days expected the sun to shine forever.

The Crash

October 29, 1929, yeah. A frenzy. I must have gotten calls from a dozen and a half friends who were desperate. In each case, there was no sense in loaning them the money that they would give the broker. Tomorrow they'd be worse off than yesterday. Suicides, left and right, made a terrific impression on me, of course. People I knew. It was heartbreaking. One day you saw the prices at a hundred, the next day at $20, at $15.

On Wall Street, the people walked around like zombies. It was like *Death Takes A Holiday* [movie from 1934]. It was very dark. You saw people who yesterday rode around in Cadillacs lucky now to have carfare.

One of my friends said to me, "If things keep on as they are, we'll all have to go begging." I asked, "Who from?"

Many brokers did not lose money. They made fortunes on commissions while their customers went broke. The only brokers that got hurt badly were those that gambled on their own—or failed to sell out in time customers' accounts that were underwater. Of course, the brokerage business fell off badly, and practically all pulled in their belts, closed down offices and threw people out of work.

Banks used to get eighteen percent for call money— money with which to buy stock that paid perhaps one or two-percent dividends. They figured the price would continue to rise. Everybody was banking on it. I used to receive as much as twenty-two percent from brokers who borrowed from me. Twenty-two percent for money!

Men who built empires in utilities would buy a small utility, add a big profit to it for themselves and sell it back to their own public company. That's how some like Samuel Insull became immensely wealthy. The thing that caused the Insull crash is the same that caused all these frenzied financiers to go broke. No matter how much they had, they'd pyramid it for more.

Meet Jessie Livermore

I had a great friend, John Hertz. At one time he owned ninety percent of the Yellow Cab stock. John also owned the Checker Cab. He also owned the Surface Line buses of Chicago. He was reputed to be worth $400 to $500 million. He asked me one day to join him on a yacht. There I met two men of such stature that I was in awe: Durant and Jesse Livermore.

We talked of all their holdings. Livermore said: "I own what I believe to be the controlling stock of IBM and Philip Morris." So I asked, "Why do you bother with anything else?" He answered, "I only understand stock. I can't bother with businesses." So I asked, "Do men of your kind put away $10 million where nobody can ever touch it?" He looked at me and answered, "Young man, what's the use of having $10 million if you can't have big money?"

In 1934—after he went through two bankruptcies in succession—my accountant asked if I'd back Livermore. He was broke and wanted to make a comeback in the market. He always made a comeback and paid everybody off with interest. I agreed to do it. I put up $400,000. By 1939, we made enough money so that each of us could have $1,300,000 profit after taxes. Jesse was, by this time in the late sixties, having gone through two bankruptcies. "Wouldn't it be wise to cash in?" I asked him. In those days, you could live like a king for $50,000 a year. He said he could just never get along on a pittance.

So I sold out, took my profits, and left Jesse on his own. He kept telling me he was going to make the killing of the century. Ben Smith, known as "Sell 'Em Short Ben," was in Europe and told him there was not going to be a war. Believing in Smith, Livermore went short on grain.[1] For every dollar he owned, plus everything he could pyramid.

When I arrived in Argentina, I learned that Germany invaded Poland. Poor Jesse was on the phone. "Art, you have to save me." I refused to do anything, being so far away. I knew it would be throwing good money after bad.

A couple of months later, I was back in New York, with Jesse waiting for me in my office. The poor fellow had lost everything he could lay his hands on. He asked for a $5,000 loan, which, of course, I gave him. Three days later, Jesse had gone to eat breakfast in the Sherry-Netherlands, went to the lavatory and shot himself. They found a note made out to me for $5,000. This was the man who said, "What's the use having ten million if you can't have big money?" Jesse was one of the most brilliant minds in the trading world. He knew the crops of every area where grain grew. He was a great student, but always overoptimistic.

Did you sense the Crash coming in 1929? I recognized it in May and saved myself a lot of money. I sold a good deal of my stocks in May. It was a case of becoming frightened. But, of course, I did not sell out completely, and finished with a very substantial loss.

In 1927 when I read [American aviator Charles] Lindbergh was planning his memorable flight, I bought Wright Aeronautic stock. He was going to fly in a plane I heard was made by Wright. I lived in Milwaukee then. My office was about a mile from my home. When I left my house, I checked with my broker. By the time I reached my office, I had made sixty-five points. The idea of everything moving so fast was frightening. Everything you bought just seemed to have no ceiling.

People say we're getting a repetition of 1929. I don't see how it is possible. Today with SEC [Securities and Ex-

1. "Selling short is selling something you don't have and buying it back in order to cover it. You think a stock is not worth what it's selling for, say it's listed as $100. You sell a hundred shares of it, though you haven't got the stock. If you are right, and it goes down to $85, you buy it at that price, and deliver it to the fellow to whom you sold it for $100. You sell what you don't have." Obviously, if the stock rises in value, selling short is ruinous. . . . Ben Smith sold short during the Crash and made "a fortune."

change Commission] controls and bank insurance, people know their savings are safe. If everybody believes, it's like believing in counterfeit money. Until it's caught, it serves its purpose.

One of the Lucky Ones

In 1932 I came to New York to open an office in the Flatiron Building. Macfadden, the health faddist, created penny restaurants. There was a Negro chap I took a liking to that I had to deal with. He agreed to line up seventy-five people who needed to be fed. At six o'clock I would leave my office, I'd march seventy-five of 'em into the Macfadden restaurant and I'd feed 'em for seven cents apiece. I did this every day. It was just unbelievable, the bread lines. The only thing I could compare it with was Germany in 1922. It looked like there was no tomorrow.

I remember the Bank Holiday. I was one of the lucky ones. I had a smart brother-in-law, an attorney. One day he said to me, "I don't feel comfortable about the bank situation. I think we ought to have a lot of cash." About eight weeks before the bank closings, we decided to take every dollar out of the banks. We must have taken out close to a million dollars. In Clyde, Ohio, where I had a porcelain enamel plant, they used my signature for money. I used to come in every Saturday and Sunday and deliver the cash. I would go around the department stores that I knew in Milwaukee and give them thirty-day IOU's of $1.05 for a dollar if they would give me cash.

In 1933, the night [gangster] Jake Factor, "The Barber," was kidnapped, an associate of mine, his wife, and a niece from Wyoming were dancing in a night club. Each of us had $25,000 cash in our socks. We were leaving the following morning for Clyde, and I was supposed to bring in $100,000 to meet bills and the payroll. We were all dancing on $25,000 apiece. In the very place where Jake Factor was kidnapped for $100,000. The damn fools, they could have grabbed us and had the cash.

Business as Usual

William Benton

Even after the stock market crash it was business as usual for some. There was always a demand for products and services and a need to advertise them. William Benton made his fortune during the Depression. He and a partner started an advertising agency that became the sixth largest agency in the world due to his innovations in advertiser-sponsored radio programs. Benton later went on to become the publisher of Encyclopedia Britannica from 1943–1971, U.S. assistant secretary of state in 1945, and a U.S. senator for Connecticut from 1949–1952.

I left Chicago in June of '29, just a few months before the Crash. Chester Bowles [at one time, Governor of Connecticut; later, American Ambassador to India] and I started in business with seventeen hundred square feet, just the two of us and a couple of girls. July 15, 1929—this was the very day of the all-time peak on the stock market.

As I solicited business, my chart was kind of a cross. The left-hand line started at the top corner and ended in the bottom of the right-hand corner. That was the stock market index. The other line was Benton & Bowles. It started at the bottom left-hand corner and ended in the top right-hand corner. A cross. As the stock market plummeted into oblivion, Benton & Bowles went up into stardom. When I sold the agency in 1935, it was the single biggest office in the world. And the most profitable office.

My friend, Beardsley Ruml, was advocate of the theory:

progress through catastrophe. In all catastrophes, there is the potential of benefit. I benefited out of the Depression. Others did, too. I suppose the people who sold red ink, red pencils and red crayons benefited.

I was only twenty-nine, and Bowles was only twenty-eight. When things are prosperous, big clients are not likely to listen to young men or to new ideas. In 1929, most of your Wall Street manipulators called it The New Era. They felt it was the start of a perpetual boom that would carry us on and on forever to new plateaus.

Surviving the Crash

That year, the sales of Pepsodent [toothpaste] were off fifty percent. Dentists talked about Pepsodent teeth. It was too abrasive, took the enamel off teeth, they said. None of the old-type advertising seemed to work. I was still in Chicago, with Lord and Thomas. Pepsodent was our account.

In May of 1929, I left my office in the new Palmolive Building . . . we were its first tenants. I walked home to my apartment. It was a hot muggy night. All the windows were open, and I heard these colored voices leaping out into the street, from all the apartments. I turned around and walked back up the street. There were nineteen radios on and seventeen were tuned to "Amos and Andy" [one of the most popular radio shows of all time]. This is probably the first audience research survey in the history of radio broadcasting.

I went in to see Mr. [Albert] Lasker [manager of Lord and Thomas] the next morning and said we ought to buy "Amos and Andy" for Pepsodent right away. We bought them on the spot, and I went east to Benton & Bowles.

Pepsodent went on the air, and within a series of weeks it was the greatest sensation in the history of American show business. The only thing that's been more famous than "Amos and Andy" was [aviator Charles] Lindbergh's flight across the Atlantic. Pepsodent sales skyrocketed.

The Crash never hurt Pepsodent. Pepsodent sales doubled and quadrupled. It was sold to Lever Brothers at an enor-

Those Directly Affected

While the stock market crash took its immediate toll on wealthy investors, the effect quickly trickled down to the average worker. The following excerpt is taken from Gordon Parks's autobiography, A Choice of Weapons. *Parks was sixteen years old in 1929 and a bellboy at an exclusive club in Minnesota. When the crash came, his whole life changed. In later years, Parks went on to become an author, photographer, and film director.*

The employees' locker room at the club was unusually quiet when I arrived at work on Wednesday. Waiters who had known each other for years were sitting about as though they were strangers. The cause of the silence was tacked to the bulletin board. It read: "Because of unforeseen circumstances, some personnel will be laid off the first of next month. Those directly affected will be notified in due time. The management."

"That Hoover's ruining the country," an old waiter finally said. No one answered him. I changed into my suit of blue tails, wondering what had happened.

By Thursday the entire world knew. "MARKET CRASHES—PANIC HITS NATION!" one headline blared. The newspapers were full of it, and I read everything I could get my hands on, gathering in the full meaning of such terms as Black Thursday, deflation and depression. I couldn't imagine such financial disaster touching my small world; it surely concerned only the rich. But by the first week of November I too knew differently; along with millions of others across the nation, I was without a job. All that next week I searched for any kind of work that would prevent my leaving school. Again it was, "We're firing, not hiring." "Sorry, sonny, nothing doing here." Finally, on the seventh of November I went to school and cleaned out my locker, knowing it was impossible to stay on. A piercing chill was in the air as I walked back to the rooming house. The hawk had come. I could already feel his wings shadowing me.

Gordon Parks, *A Choice of Weapons*. New York: Harper & Row, 1966.

mous price, giving Lasker part of his great fortune. Benton & Bowles plunged into radio in a big way for our clients.

The Depression Passed Me Over

We didn't know the Depression was going on. Except that our clients' products were plummeting, and they were willing to talk to us about new ideas. They wouldn't have let us in the door if times were good. So the Depression benefited me. My income doubled every year. When I left Benton & Bowles, it must have been close to half a million dollars. That's the kind of money great motion picture stars weren't earning. That was 1935. The Depression just passed me right over. I'm not a good man to talk to about the Depression.

I had nothing to do with the creation of "Amos and Andy," just had the judgment to buy it. But I contributed enormously to the "Maxwell House Show Boat," which later became the Number One program in broadcasting. The show gave a quality of illusion to the radio audiences so perfectly that in its early weeks ten thousand and fifteen thousand people would come down to the docks in Memphis and Nashville, where we said the "Show Boat" was going to tie up.

"Show Boat" went on in 1933, really the bottom of the Depression. Maxwell House Coffee went up eighty-five percent within six months. And kept zooming. Thus, Maxwell House didn't know there was a Depression. The chain stores were selling coffee that was almost as good—the difference was indetectable—for a much lower price. But advertising so gave glamor and verve to Maxwell House that it made everybody think it was a whale of a lot better. It doubled and quadrupled in sales.

In "Show Boat" we did something nobody had ever done before. We cast two people in one role. We'd get a sexy singer, who might not be a good actress, then we'd get the sexiest actress we could find and we'd give her the speaking lines, softening the audience up, getting it warm and ready to melt. Then the girl would come in and sing. . . .

We went on to put out other shows like it. And they became big hits. "The Palmolive Beauty Box." I picked up an unknown member of the Metropolitan chorus, Gladys Swarthout, and we made her a big star. We put a $100-a-week gifted actress with her to speak the lines, while Gladys sang in that seductive voice of hers. They told me I couldn't use her because she was no soprano and the parts were too high. I just coolly said: rewrite the parts; write them lower. Nobody in opera would have thought of this. . . . We succeeded in radio because none of us knew any better.

These were the new techniques of the Depression. As their sales went off, the big advertisers looked around and said: Who are these new young men that have these new ideas that appeal to these new young people? We looked like college boys, and yet they paid us a great deal of money. This is why Chet Bowles and I escaped the Depression.

The type of men that largely dominated advertising, before the Depression, faded—the ones who played golf with their accounts. The Depression speeded up greatly the use of research in marketing. I developed new techniques, working for Lasker, which I took East with me. [Public opinion statistician] George Gallup brought in new standards. He once referred to me as his grandfather, because I pioneered in the advertising field . . . finding out what the consumers wanted.

The Maxwell House Coffee program was, to my eternal regret, the stimulus that changed the commercials. When we had Captain Andy drink coffee and smack his lips, you heard the coffee cups clinking and the coffee gurgling as it was poured. It put action and actors into commercials. That was a revolution, the full import of which we didn't suspect at the time. It inevitably led to the singing commercial and all the current excesses. As Bob Hutchins [president of the University of Chicago 1928–1951] said, when he introduced me at a dinner in my honor at the University of Chicago— I invented things that I now apologize for.

Marketing a Habit-Forming Product

I presumably lost $150,000 in the depression of 1937—on my one stock investment—because I did everything Lehman Brothers told me. I said, well, this is a fool's procedure . . .

buying stock in other people's businesses. I'll have to buy my own company. I won't work at operating it, I'll just own it. I'll set the policies. I looked around and bought the Muzak Corporation. I never could have bought it except in a Depression. It was a busted, rundown company. That would be around '38.

Muzak was then only heard in hotels and restaurants in New York. It was only thought of as a substitute for live music. Jimmy Petrillo cursed it as the Number One enemy of musicians. I said to myself: This music ought to be in other places.

I went down to see the five salesmen—we only had five then. They said to me: "We have eighty percent of all the business you can get in New York. There isn't any other place to sell it." I said, "Why don't you put it in barber shops and doctors' offices?" "Oh, you can't put Muzak in places like that!" I said: "Do you all five think that way?" There was a young man, who had only worked there six weeks, he said "No, I think it's a good idea." I said, "Well, the other four of you guys had better quit and get some other jobs, and I'll make this young man the sales manager. We'll take Muzak into new areas."

Of course, this made a big wonderful business out of Muzak, now earning $2 million a year. And no extra money has ever gone into it. The Depression put me into it.

The first installation outside the customary public for music was a bank in New York. The manager said, "My people who work at night, it's very depressing in these electric-lit offices. They wanted a radio, but I didn't want them to have it. I told them I'd give them Muzak. Now it's all over the bank." There was a girl sitting as a receptionist in the personal loan department. That's where people would borrow money in small units and never come back unless they couldn't pay the installments. The girl said to me: "The music makes this place less gruesome."

I invented the phrase: "Music not to be listened to." That was my commercial phrase with which I sold Muzak. It was the first music deliberately created to which people were not supposed to listen. It was a new kind of background music. That's why my mother, who was a fine musician, held it in contempt. She wouldn't have it in her apartment. Anybody who knows anything about music holds Muzak in contempt.

I have a tin ear. That's why my ear was so good for radio. Most people in the United States have a tin ear like mine. A totally tin ear. I really like Rudy Vallee and Bing Crosby and the stars that were developed by radio.

I owned Muzak for twenty years and sold it for a profit of many millions . . . when I ran out of my first million and needed some more.

Muzak's habit-forming. The man who bought it from me gave me four installations for my homes and my offices. I always have it on. 'Cause I notice it when it's not on and don't notice it when it's on. That's how it's music not to be listened to. And that's how it's habit-forming.

Every businessman wants a product that is habit-forming. That's why cigarettes, Coca-Cola and coffee do so well. Even soap is habit-forming. Soaps were my biggest products when I was in the agency business.

Getting Out of Advertising

I always thought—at Benton & Bowles—just six more months, three more, and it would all be behind me. But our business doubled every year. Every year, I would say: As soon as I get this new client, I won't be working like this. No intelligent man would put up with what I put up with, even to get a million dollars, if he could have foreseen the six years.

Chapter 2

Out of Work, Out of Luck

Chapter Preface

The Depression didn't seem so bad in the beginning. Hoover had predicted that the crisis would be short-lived and that the economy would be back to where it was before the crash. But when the weeks dragged on into months and the months turned into years, people began to realize that the Depression would not be as easily remedied as their president had foretold. At the peak of the Depression, a quarter of the population was put out of work. A million people were unemployed in New York alone. Some cities like Detroit experienced unemployment rates of more than 50 percent. Minorities and women experienced the worst discrimination and composed a large number of those statistics. Jobs that were typically held by African Americans before the crash were given to white employees after it. And when African Americans and women did manage to find jobs, they were paid far less than their white counterparts. Married women could not find jobs at all because it was considered unfair; they had husbands who were supposed to support them.

The block-long lines of men and women standing in breadlines became synonymous with the Depression. The private charities and city relief agencies of every major city did the best they could to keep people fed, despite the overwhelming numbers. Many resorted to offering half shares of food so that they could feed more people.

As the Depression deepened, businesses across the country resorted to layoffs and wage drops to survive. Longer hours and less pay made it difficult for even the fully employed to make ends meet. But nobody doubted that the people who had any job were the lucky ones. Those who weren't employed had a choice of either sitting in an unemployment office or warming a park bench, scanning the want ads. The sheer number of applicants for what few jobs were available made getting anything difficult. Overwhelmed social workers and employment counselors who had little good news to offer became as discouraged as their charges.

Governor of New York and future president Franklin Roosevelt took the lead and authorized the issuance of relief checks. New York became the first city to offer relief checks to the needy residents of the city. This act was a precursor to the New Deal that Roosevelt would implement as president; direct relief was something President Hoover refused to offer to the needy. But even a big city like New York did not have the resources to sustain relief programs for very long—especially when large numbers of destitute farmers from the country were moving to the city looking for jobs. Even with the creation of the Federal Emergency Relief Agency (FERA), which provided relief money to hard-pressed states, the local relief agencies and charities were underfunded and had to rely on a little ingenuity to keep the hungry fed.

Waiting Was the Worst Part

Meridel Le Sueur

The stock market crash of 1929 did not affect most people because not everyone had the extra money to invest. But as banks and businesses reacted to cut costs or declare bankruptcy, unemployment rose at an alarming rate. Relief organizations were quickly overwhelmed and unemployment offices were swamped with applicants. Meridel Le Sueur was a young writer who wrote the following article about what it was like for women seeking work in an employment office. She describes the frustration and humiliation of proud people waiting all day for jobs that rarely, if ever, materialized. Le Sueur went on to write several influential novels about the era.

I am sitting in the city free employment bureau. It's the women's section. We have been sitting here now for four hours. We sit here every day, waiting for a job. There are no jobs. Most of us have had no breakfast. Some have had scant rations for over a year. Hunger makes a human being lapse into a state of lethargy, especially city hunger. Is there any place else in the world where a human being is supposed to go hungry amidst plenty without an outcry, without protest, where only the boldest steal or kill for bread, and the timid crawl the streets, hunger like the beak of a terrible bird at the vitals?

We sit looking at the floor. No one dares think of the

Excerpted from "Women on the Breadlines," by Meridel Le Sueur, *New Masses*, January 1932, pp. 5–7. Reprinted with permission from Deborah Le Sueur.

coming winter. There are only a few more days of summer. Everyone is anxious to get work to lay up something for that long siege of bitter cold. But there is no work. Sitting in the room we all know it. That is why we don't talk much. We look at the floor dreading to see that knowledge in each other's eyes. There is a kind of humiliation in it. We look away from each other. We look at the floor. It's too terrible to see this animal terror in each other's eyes.

So we sit hour after hour, day after day, waiting for a job to come in. There are many women for a single job. A thin sharp woman sits inside the wire cage looking at a book. For four hours we have watched her looking at that book. She has a hard little eye. In the small bare room there are half a dozen women sitting on the benches waiting. Many come and go. Our faces are all familiar to each other, for we wait here everyday.

Women Alone

This is a domestic employment bureau. Most of the women who come here are middle-aged, some have families, some have raised their families and are now alone, some have men who are out of work. Hard times and the man leaves to hunt for work. He doesn't find it. He drifts on. The woman probably doesn't hear from him for a long time. She expects it. She isn't surprised. She struggles alone to feed the many mouths. Sometimes she gets help from the charities. If she's clever she can get herself a good living from the charities, if she's naturally a lick-spittle, naturally a little docile and cunning. If she's proud then she starves silently, leaving her children to find work, coming home after a day's searching to wrestle with her house, her children.

Some such story is written on the faces of all these women. There are young girls too, fresh from the country. Some are made brazen too soon by the city. There is a great exodus of girls from the farms into the city now. Thousands of farms have been vacated completely in Minnesota. The girls are trying to get work. The prettier ones can get jobs in the stores when there are any, or waiting on table, but these jobs are only for the attractive and the adroit, the others, the real peasants have a more difficult time.

Bernice sits next me. She is a large Polish woman of thirty-five. She has been working in peoples' kitchens for fifteen years or more. She is large, her great body in mounds, her face brightly scrubbed. She has a peasant mind and finds it hard even yet to understand the maze of the city where trickery is worth more than brawn. Her blue eyes are not clever but slow and trusting. She suffers from loneliness and lack of talk. When you speak to her her face lifts and brightens as if you had spoken through a great darkness and she talks magically of little things, as if the weather were magic or tells some crazy tale of her adventures on the city streets, embellishing them in bright colors until they hang heavy and thick like some peasant embroidery. She loves the city anyhow. It's exciting to her, like a bazaar. She loves to go shopping and get a bargain, hunting out the places where stale bread and cakes can be had for a few cents. She likes walking the streets looking for men to take her to a picture show. Sometimes she

Women march for jobs before relief administration officials in New York. Arriving in the city from farms, women faced high unemployment.

goes to five picture shows in one day, or she sits through one the entire day until she knows all the dialogue by heart.

She came to the city a young girl from a Wisconsin farm. The first thing that happened to her a charlatan dentist took out all her good shining teeth and the fifty dollars she had saved working in a canning factory. After that she met men in the park who told her how to look out for herself, corrupting her peasant mind, teaching her to mistrust everyone. Sometimes now she forgets to mistrust everyone and gets taken in. They taught her to get what she could for nothing, to count her change, to go back if she found herself cheated, to demand her rights.

She lives alone in little rooms. She bought seven dollars worth of second-hand furniture eight years ago. She rents a room for perhaps three dollars a month in an attic, sometimes in a cold house. Once the house where she stayed was condemned and everyone else moved out and she lived there all winter alone on the top floor. She spent only twenty-five dollars all winter.

She wants to get married but she sees what happens to her married friends, being left with children to support, worn out before their time. So she stays single. She is virtuous. She is slightly deaf from hanging out clothes in winter. She has done people's washings and cooking for fifteen years and in that time she saved thirty dollars. Now she hasn't worked steady for a year and she has spent the thirty dollars. She dreamed of having a little house or a houseboat perhaps with a spot of ground for a few chickens. This dream she will never realize.

She has lost all her furniture now along with the dream. A married friend whose husband is gone gives her a bed for which she pays by doing a great deal of work for the woman. She comes here every day now sitting bewildered, her pudgy hands folded in her lap. She is hungry. Her great flesh has begun to hang in folds. She has been living on crackers. Sometimes a box of crackers lasts a week. She has a friend who's a baker and he sometimes steals the stale loaves and brings them to her.

Rage Erupts

A girl we have seen every day all summer went crazy yesterday at the Y.W. She went into hysterics, stamping her feet and screaming.

She hadn't had work for eight months. "You've got to give me something," she kept saying. The woman in charge flew into a rage that probably came from days and days of suffering on her part, because she is unable to give jobs, having none. She flew into a rage at the girl and there they were facing each other in a rage both helpless, helpless. This woman told me once that she could hardly bear the suffering she saw, hardly hear it, that she couldn't eat sometimes and had nightmares at night.

So they stood there the two women in a rage, the girl weeping and the woman shouting at her. In the eight months of unemployment she had gotten ragged, and the woman was shouting that she would not send her out like that. "Why don't you shine your shoes," she kept scolding the girl, and the girl kept sobbing and sobbing because she was starving.

"We can't recommend you like that," the harrassed Y.W.C.A. woman said, knowing she was starving, unable to do anything. And the girls and the women sat docilely their eyes on the ground, ashamed to look at each other, ashamed of something.

Sitting here waiting for a job, the women have been talking in low voices about the girl Ellen. They talk in low voices with not too much pity for her, unable to see through the mist of their own torment. "What happened to Ellen?" one of them asks. She knows the answer already. We all know it.

A young girl who went around with Ellen tells about seeing her last evening back of a cafe downtown outside the kitchen door, kicking, showing her legs so that the cook came out and gave her some food, and some men gathered in the alley and threw a small coin on the ground for a look at her legs. And the girl says enviously that Ellen had a swell breakfast and treated her to one, too, that cost two dollars.

A scrub woman whose hips are bent forward from stoop-

The Idle Men

As the Depression wore on, the unemployment situation worsened. The scene became the same in every city across the nation. Thousands of idle men wandered the streets waiting for work. In the New England mill town of Lowell, Massachusetts, the closing of the local mills put two-thirds of the town out of work. Louis Adamic was a novelist and a journalist who traveled throughout New England and recorded what he saw. The following excerpt is from his book, My America.

I saw men standing on the sidewalks clapping their hands in a queer way, obviously just to be doing something. I saw men talking to themselves, walking around, stopping, looking into shop windows, walking again.

For several minutes I watched an elderly man who stood on a deserted corner near the enormous and idle Everett Mills in the posture of an undotted question mark. He did not see me. Every now and then he swung his arms, not because it was cold, but no doubt because he wanted activity other than walking around, which he probably had been doing for years in a vain effort to get a job. He mumbled to himself. Then, suddenly, he stepped off the curb and picked up a long piece of string from a pile of rubbish, and his big, work-eager hands began to work with it, tying and untying feverishly. He worked with the string for several minutes. Then he looked around and, seeing me, dropped the string, his haggard, hollow face coloring a little, as though from a sense of guilt, or intense embarrassment. He was shaken and confused and stood there for several seconds, looking down at the rubbish heap, then up at me. His hands finally dropped to his sides. Then his arms swung in a sort of idle reflex motion and he turned, hesitated a while as if he did not know where to go and finally shuffled off, flapping his arms. I noticed that his overcoat was split in the back and that his heels were worn off completely.

Louis Adamic, *My America.* New York: Harper, 1938.

ing with hands gnarled like water soaked branches clicks her tongue in disgust. No one saves their money, she says, a little money and these foolish young things buy a hat, a dollar for breakfast, a bright scarf. And they do. If you've ever been without money, or food, something very strange happens when you get a bit of money, a kind of madness. You don't care. You can't remember that you had no money before, that the money will be gone. You can remember nothing but that there is the money for which you have been suffering. Now here it is. A lust takes hold of you. You see food in the windows. In imagination you eat hugely; you taste a thousand meals. You look in windows. Colours are brighter; you buy something to dress up in. An excitement takes hold of you. You know it is suicide but you can't help it. You must have food, dainty, splendid food and a bright hat so once again you feel blithe, rid of that ratty gnawing shame.

"I guess she'll go on the street now," a thin woman says faintly and no one takes the trouble to comment further. Like every commodity now the body is difficult to sell and the girls say you're lucky if you get fifty cents.

It's very difficult and humiliating to sell one's body.

Perhaps it would make it clear if one were to imagine having to go out on the street to sell, say, one's overcoat. Suppose you have to sell your coat so you can have breakfast and a place to sleep, say, for fifty cents. You decide to sell your only coat. You take it off and put it on your arm. The street, that has before been just a street, now becomes a mart, something entirely different. You must approach someone now and admit you are destitute and are now selling your clothes, your most intimate possessions. Everyone will watch you talking to the stranger showing him your overcoat, what a good coat it is. People will stop and watch curiously. You will be quite naked on the street. It is even harder to try and sell one's self, more humiliating. It is even humiliating to try and sell one's labour. When there is no buyer.

The thin woman opens the wire cage. There's a job for a nursemaid, she says. The old gnarled women, like old horses, know that no one will have them walk the streets with the young so they don't move. Ellen's friend gets up and goes to the window. She is unbelievably jaunty. I know she hasn't had work since last January. But she has a flare of life in her that glows like a tiny red flame and some tenacious thing, perhaps only youth, keeps it burning bright. Her legs are thin but the runs in her old stockings are neatly mended clear down her flat shank. Two bright spots of rouge conceal her palor. A narrow belt is drawn tightly around her thin waist, her long shoulders stoop and the blades show. She runs wild as a colt hunting pleasure, hunting sustenance.

Where Do the Homeless Women Go?

It's one of the great mysteries of the city where women go when they are out of work and hungry. There are not many women in the bread line. There are no flop houses for women as there are for men, where a bed can be had for a quarter or less. You don't see women lying on the floor at the mission in the free flops. They obviously don't sleep in the jungle or under newspapers in the park. There is no law I suppose against their being in these places but the fact is they rarely are.

Yet there must be as many women out of jobs in cities and suffering extreme poverty as there are men. What happens to them? Where do they go? Try to get into the Y.W. without any money or looking down at heel. Charities take care of very few and only those that are called "deserving." The lone girl is under suspicion by the virgin women who dispense charity.

I've lived in cities for many months broke, without help, too timid to get in bread lines. I've known many women to live like this until they simply faint on the street from privations, without saying a word to anyone. A woman will shut herself up in a room until it is taken away from her, and eat a cracker a day and be as quiet as a mouse so there are no social statistics concerning her.

I don't know why it is, but a woman will do this unless she has dependents, will go for weeks verging on starvation, crawling in some hole, going through the streets ashamed, sitting in libraries, parks, going for days without speaking to a living soul like some exiled beast, keeping the runs mended in her stockings, shut up in terror in her own misery, until she becomes too supersensitive and timid to even ask for a job.

Bernice says even strange men she has met in the park have sometimes, that is in better days, given her a loan to pay her room rent. She has always paid them back.

In the afternoon the young girls, to forget the hunger and the deathly torture and fear of being jobless, try and pick up a man to take them to a ten-cent show. They never go to more expensive ones, but they can always find a man willing to spend a dime to have the company of a girl for the afternoon.

Sometimes a girl facing the night without shelter will approach a man for lodging. A woman always asks a man for help. Rarely another woman. I have known girls to sleep in men's rooms for the night, on a pallet without molestation, and given breakfast in the morning.

It's no wonder these young girls refuse to marry, refuse to rear children. They are like certain savage tribes, who, when they have been conquered, refuse to breed.

Not one of them but looks forward to starvation, for the coming winter. We are in a jungle and know it. We are beaten, entrapped. There is no way out. Even if there were a job, even if that thin acrid woman came and gave everyone in the room a job for a few days, a few hours, at thirty cents an hour, this would all be repeated tomorrow, the next day and the next.

Not one of these women but knows, that despite years of labour there is only starvation, humiliation in front of them.

A Woman Drowning

Mrs. Grey, sitting across from me, is a living spokesman for the futility of labour. She is a warning. Her hands are scarred with labour. Her body is a great puckered scar. She has given birth to six children, buried three, supported them all alive and dead, bearing them, burying them, feeding them. Bred in hunger they have been spare, susceptible to disease.

For seven years she tried to save her boy's arm from amputation, diseased from tuberculosis of the bone. It is almost too suffocating to think of that long close horror of years of child bearing, child feeding, rearing, with the bare suffering of providing a meal and shelter.

Now she is fifty. Her children, economically insecure, are drifters. She never hears of them. She doesn't know if they are alive. She doesn't know if she is alive. Such subtleties of suffering are not for her. For her the brutality of hunger and cold, the bare bone of life. That is enough. These will occupy a life. Not until these are done away with can those subtle feelings that make a human being be indulged.

She is lucky to have five dollars ahead of her. That is her security. She has a tumour that she will die of. She is thin as a worn dime with her tumour sticking out of her side. She is brittle and bitter. Her face is not the face of a human being. She has born more than it is possible for a human being to bear. She is reduced to the least possible denominator of human feelings.

It is terrible to see her little bloodshot eyes like a beaten hound's, fearful in terror.

We cannot meet her eyes. When she looks at any of us we look away. She is like a woman drowning and we turn away. We must ignore those eyes that are surely the eyes of a person drowning, doomed. She doesn't cry out. She goes down decently. And we all look away.

The young ones know though. I don't want to marry. I don't want any children. So they all say. No children. No marriage. They arm themselves alone, keep up alone. The man is helpless now. He cannot provide. If he propagates he cannot take care of his young. The means are not in his hands. So they live alone. Get what fun they can. The life risk is too horrible now. Defeat is too clearly written on it.

So we sit in this room like cattle, waiting for a nonexistent job, willing to work to the farthest atom of energy, unable to work, unable to get food and lodging, unable to bear children; here we must sit in this shame looking at the floor, worse than beasts at a slaughter.

It is appalling to think that these women sitting so list-less in the room may work as hard as it is possible for a human being to work, may labour night and day, like Mrs. Gray wash street cars from midnight to dawn and offices in the early evening, scrubbing for fourteen and fifteen hours a day, sleeping only five hours or so, doing this their whole lives, and never earn one day of security, having always before them the pit of the future. The endless labour, the bending back, the water soaked hands, earning never more than a week's wages, never having in their hands more life than that.

It's not the suffering, not birth, death, love that the young reject, but the suffering of endless labour without dream, eating the spare bread in bitterness, a slave without the security of a slave.

The Grandest Hooverville of Them All

W.W. Waters

In 1932, an estimated fifteen to twenty-five thousand veterans
of the First World War converged on Washington, D.C., to
demand bonuses that had been promised to them by Congress.
The bonuses were actually scheduled to be paid in 1945. But
like much of the country, the veterans were unemployed and
having a difficult time making ends meet. The bonus with
interest would average a thousand dollars per recipient. This
much money could go a long way in the 1930s.

The veterans called themselves the Bonus Expeditionary
Force (BEF), which was a parody of the U.S. American Expeditionary Force that had been sent to Europe during the First
World War. The BEF was led by a former army medic named
Walter Waters who had been laid off from a cannery several
years before. Waters began the march in Portland, Oregon,
but BEF members hitchhiked and hopped freight trains from
all over the country. They set up camp all over Washington,
D.C., in abandoned buildings and encampments along an inlet
of the Potomac River in Anacostia.

The ragged, makeshift camp—like other transient encampments that sprang up in America's cities—was known as a
Hooverville, mocking the name of the president who seemed
incapable of relieving the plight of the jobless. The following
excerpt is taken from Waters's autobiography that was written

Excerpted from *B.E.F.: The Whole Story of the Bonus Army* (New York: John Day
Company, 1933) by W.W. Waters as told to William C. White. Copyright © 1933 by W.W.
Waters and William C. White.

with the help of William C. White. He describes the conditions in the biggest BEF encampment, Camp Marks, named after a local police captain. He also describes how Police Chief Pelham G. Glassford selflessly helped the veterans obtain what they needed to live.

Unfortunately, the resolution for early payment did not pass so the veterans did not get their money. Most of the veterans packed up and left Washington disappointed, but two thousand to five thousand men remained and staged protests over the next few weeks. Eventually, President Hoover intervened and ordered General Douglas MacArthur to remove protesters from their encampments. But MacArthur took an iron-handed approach and drove the veterans out of the city using tanks and tear gas. One veteran was killed and several police officers were wounded during the eviction.

A broad, level field lay on the bank of an inlet of the Potomac. A long drawbridge over a narrow arm of greasy water connected it with the city proper. Never had the field looked particularly habitable. Any rain that fell collected in puddles and the neighborhood boys that used the field for a ball park slid around in the mud. The field was under the jurisdiction of the Park Commissioners who hoped to make an attractive playground out of it some day. But it looked unhealthy, that flat strip of river bank running down to the sluggish, oil-sheeted waters of the inlet. Some years ago, before the Department of Health had been well organized, it had been a malaria area. Smoky swarms of mosquitoes droned over it at nightfall.

In the middle of June, two weeks later, that field at Anacostia looked like a cross between a Congo village, a trash pile, a picnic ground and a tourist camp. Ten thousand men were living on it, a thousand men to an acre. In well-run military camps, the total capacity of an acre is set at three hundred. They were washing and bathing in the river and suffering from boils a few days later. Two fire hose ran pure water into the settlement to be carried in any kind of containers to the huts. The warm wind blew the acrid odor of quicklime and chloride into the faces of the thousands of visitors who passed by the military guard at the entrances. Middle June was rainy, and the thousands of passing feet churned the field into a morass. The men walked around in bare feet. The visiting health officers used boots. The mud was bad enough to have to walk through. Ten thousand men knew that sleeping in it was worse.

Setting Up Camp

The arrival of a particularly large group, from Camden, New Jersey, precipitated the problem of an outdoor encampment for the B.E.F. General Glassford [former general and current chief of police] secured permission from the Park Commissioners to use Anacostia Field. As he said later, the idea of being able to raise the drawbridges and to cut the main body of the B.E.F. off from the city proper appealed to him. The first men marched on Anacostia on June 4th. Here tragedy was soon to stalk; here the election of 1932 was to be lost by the Republican party.

Anacostia Field soon showed how ten thousand men, penniless and with little more than the clothes that they wore and their discharge papers, would provide a shelter for themselves. But tents and shelter were not as important as having something other than the ground to lie on. Dismantled automobile bodies, considered the choicest of all treasures to be salvaged from junk heaps, ancient double-decker bed frames, with boards stretched across them, bags of dried grass—these kept sleeping men out of the mud. General Glassford later secured a small quantity of bed ticks and straw, and they, too, were soon spread over Anacostia. Some of the men dug caves in the clay banks behind the field and slept there. One man found a casket and set it on trestles for his bed. Another found a piano box and put up a sign, "Academy Of Music."

Anything that could be put upright served for walls and roofs. Packing boxes, even of cardboard, and sheets of plaited grass plucked in nearby fields, served when no more boards could be found. The reed roofs added an air, half Barnum, half Congo, to the village in its first days. Later more permanent structures of lumber were erected. One man, an ex-attorney, graduated from Cornell, built a model cottage of stucco blocks. Two negroes, one from New York, the other from Detroit, took the names of Abe Goldstein and Cohen, and opened rival second-hand stores and, prophetically enough, announced fire sales. A few hopeful individuals started vegetable gardens, but not with free government seed.[1]

A World War I veteran and his family join thousands of others in the Anacostia encampment in Washington, D.C., to demand bonuses promised by Congress.

It may sound crude, but here was a home even when folded newspapers, from which beef stew dripped, had to serve as plates. Anacostia, in furnishing some sense of security, even temporary, was answering the very need that had brought these thousands to Washington. For most of the

1. Early Depression aid from President Hoover was the distribution of fruit and vegetable seeds to needy families.

men, home on Anacostia Field had some novelty. No land-lords came daily threatening eviction. No bill collectors called. There was no need to fear the imperious ring of the doorbell. The absence of gas and electricity had at least the compensating comfort that neither could be cut off for non-payment of bills.

The camp at Anacostia was later called Camp Marks, in honor of Captain Marks, of a nearby police station, who helped us in every way.

Ten days after the first occupation of Anacostia came the first rainy night. An inspection detail went around the camp. "All hands are sheltered somehow," one officer reported, "but damn few feet are!"

General Glassford brought some lumber and a few large wall-less shelters were built. Each of the groups that settled on the field soon organized a "Lumber Chiseling Squad," whose members roamed the city and searched the ash-piles for anything that might be used to provide a bit more shelter than the stars.

Sanitary arrangements were at first very simple here, as in every other billet, and were never completely satisfactory. There was a good deal of dysentery and an epidemic of sore feet, but no other epidemic arose. The fact that all of the men had been inoculated during the War may have helped prevent typhoid. The custom of bathing in the river was soon stopped and some few shower baths erected. There was only one shower, however, for each seven hundred men. The men were amazingly eager to keep clean, considering the effort it took. The old army habit of forcibly cleaning up any individual too lazy to do so for himself soon returned. Our old Army friends, the cooties, joined us. Those veterans in the camp who had had some experience in Red Cross work during the War opened a dispensary. Later physicians were detailed to the camps from the Health Department. The Health Department was faced with various problems—from investigating food poisoning outbreaks to taking care of mothers in childbirth.

The men camped at Anacostia, as at all other billets, jealously preserved their State groupings. At Anacostia most of the men had come from the Eastern States. Some of the groups, from various cities, kept separate identities. The New York City group even maintained, separately, a "Hell's Kitchen" unit and a unit from the East Side that rarely mixed. The negroes from the North were not particularly willing to mix with the negroes from the South. The preservation of State and locality divisions made identification and control of the men somewhat simpler. Occasionally the custom had its drawbacks. The men from the States and cities near Washington would receive trucks of foodstuffs from home and refuse to divide them with the men from more distant points. Then, when we ruled that such division was arbitrary and forbade trucks being sent directly into Anacostia Field, the home folks refused to send any more food, "If our own boys can't keep it!"

The men who were quartered in the semi-dilapidated buildings in various parts of the city had at least a shelter overhead. The least uncomfortable of all were the men at Camp Bartlett, six miles from the center of the city. The shelters here were National Guard tents.

The problem of food was met at first by the money in General Glassford's care.[2] Later, we had to depend more and more on donations. Army kitchens, which General Glassford personally borrowed from the National Guard, were assigned to each unit and we tried to serve two meals a day, and if lucky, three. We managed during the entire time to furnish bread and coffee as a minimum and never once failed. The rest of the menu varied from turtle soup to boiled grits. Only by the narrowest margin on one or two days in July was sufficient food secured to prevent a foodless day. Never was there food in plenty.

"This camp oughta be called 'No Seconds'" was a remark that sums up the entire food situation. One day there would have been no "firsts" if a manufacturer in New York had not

2. Glassford set up a fund of private donations of which he contributed $115 of his own money.

supplied fifteen hundred pounds of meat that was sent down by airplane.

Whole Families Arrive

The whole problem of billeting and feeding the men took on a new complexity when men began to arrive with their wives and children. They came against my advice. In addresses to the men and in letters sent all over the country the veterans were urged to leave their families at home. Yet, by the end of June, there were two hundred and twenty wives and children attached to the B.E.F. At the time of the eviction there were four hundred children and seven hundred women. They came and shared the life with their men. Their coming, although unwise, was understandable. Many of them had been evicted from their homes and had less shelter in their own communities than Anacostia furnished. Therefore, why not come and share the bit of hope about the Bonus and the meager rations? Some of the families had six and seven children. The roster sheets reported one morning some new arrivals: ". . . and the O'Brien family with six children, all redheaded and mean as hell!"

The Red Cross refused to furnish milk and proper food for the children of the B.E.F. Perhaps such a demand did not come strictly within the definition of an emergency and perhaps free milk might have attracted other women with children who were getting no milk in their local communities. Perhaps! But the kids that played in the mud of Anacostia and who were dragged by hysterical parents out of the range of low-lying clouds of tear gas on the night of the eviction could not understand the statement made a few months before by Secretary Wilbur of President Hoover's Cabinet, in speaking of the effects of the depression: "Personally, I think that our children are apt to profit rather than suffer from what is now going on."

When an "emergency" did arise the Red Cross did not fail! Although they refused to provide milk for the children yet when two babies died of stomach complaint from lack of proper diet and, later, when one died from the effects of tear gas, the Red Cross most charitably contributed the money for the little white caskets and for transportation "home." No wonder some of the members of the B.E.F. suggested jocularly that since our children, living, could get no help from American institutions, we might petition Moscow to send us help, as once we had sent help to Russian children.

An Ordered Society

The men in the various camps and billets were checked every day but it was almost impossible to keep an accurate register with the steady flow of new and unannounced arrivals and departures. But shelter and meals could be had only on presentation of discharge papers. It was almost impossible for any non-veterans to use the B.E.F. as a meal ticket. The president of the "Hoboes of America" wrote me, thoughtfully, to say that he had ordered all tramps to stay out of Washington in order to give the B.E.F. a chance.

During the first weeks no attempt was made to direct the activities of the men during the day. Only at the end of June did we introduce military drill. The only restrictions we put on the men were "no drinking" and "no speech making by unauthorized persons." During the first days half of the orators in Washington, no matter what their subject or purpose, tried to plead, implore, cajole, and, too often, to sell something to the B.E.F. Political candidates for all offices thought they saw a chance to drum up a few votes. We finally issued an order: "No speeches to the B.E.F. except on the Bonus and immediately related problems."

The men at Anacostia were free to come and go as they wished. Each outfit organized its own details, to gather wood, to clean up the place, and to perform various other duties, but there was nothing to prevent some easily tired member of the detail saying: "Can't work today. I gotta go see a Congressman!"

In spite of strict orders against individual panhandling, "chiseling," the practice could not be stopped and slowly increased until it provided one of the reasons for eventually dissolving the B.E.F. Most of it went on under the surface and the B.E.F. headquarters knew little of it. The B.E.F. naturally attracted some men who made "chiseling" their profession; the reputation of the B.E.F. did not increase by their presence and their practice. Some of the outfits, rather surreptitiously, organized their "chiseling details" in, elaborate fashion. The chaps who could secure just a bit of food for themselves were "ordinary chiselers." Those who managed to bring back more than they needed were "advanced." Those of the highest rank, who could secure something particularly necessary to the camp, especially money, were titled "promoters."

"I met a guy downtown and I managed to 'promote' a roll of tar paper," was one proud boast.

Too frequently, faithful attendance at the Senate building or in other public offices was not so much for political purpose as it was to "promote" a cake of soap or some paper towels from the washrooms.

Against such panhandling and "promoting" every outfit was continually warned. We tried especially to keep men from soliciting around town and pocketing the returns for their own use. The sale of the B.E.F. newspaper, started in June, was begun largely to help the men earn a little money so that they might not feel entirely penniless.

In contrast to this practice in the B.E.F. there is one proud record. After two weeks in camp the only crime against property reported in the whole B.E.F. was that of one negro who was charged by an old lady with having taken slats from her fence. In the course of our seven weeks in Washington including the day of eviction, the police reported 362 arrests of men in the B.E.F., of which twelve were for "actual criminal offenses."

Beyond co-operating with the local police, if it should be necessary, we leaders were powerless to enforce our decrees if the men did not wish. After all, we had no way of inflicting punishment on any legitimate veterans for insubordination. "We aren't in the army now," someone reminded me each day. They "groused" steadily, at any chance. One man even complained about the luxury of turtle soup aforementioned. "They mighta sent us enough turtles so we coulda had seconds," he complained. Noncommissioned officers, particularly, know that, like a dog's wet nose, such "beefing" is a sign of health. Our record of discipline can be summed up in one sentence: not once, in the history of the B.E.F. in Washington did the local police have to make an arrest of their own volition on B.E.F. grounds. Some arrests were made by our military police, chiefly for possessing liquor, and the prisoner turned over to the District authorities.

Them That Needs

Slim Jackson

> During the Depression there was a lot of controversy sur-
> rounding relief and how it should be distributed. President
> Hoover and other conservatives believed it wasn't the gov-
> ernment's function to issue handouts. That mentality came in
> conflict with President Roosevelt's New Deal programs that
> tried to provide aid directly to the people. Slim Jackson
> worked for Roosevelt's Works Progress Administration
> (WPA) distributing relief supplies. In the following WPA
> writer's project account recorded by Della Yoe and Jennette
> Edwards, Jackson describes his opinions about relief, the
> people he's met in the relief lines, and the trials his own
> family has experienced.

The way I look at it is this. This is a rich country. I figger
it ain't going to hurt the government to feed and clothe
them that needs it. Half of 'em can't get work, or just ain't
fixed to handle work if they get it. I imagine this country's
worth near on to ten billion dollars. We've got the money.
Plenty of it. No sense in the big fellows kicking about a little handout to the poor. Matter's not if some ain't deserving.

I'll admit there's some don't deserve a nickel of the government's money. Lot of them that comes here, why I'd
sooner give them a kick in the pants than shove 'em out supplies. But you got to take the good with the bad. Or bad with
the good, whichever way you've a mind to put it. Most that
comes here are poor and can't help it. Needs help. Needs it
just same I need this job. Always going to be more poor

folks than them that ain't poor. Now take me. I've always been poor and I guess I always will be. I ain't saying that's the government's fault. It's just a downright truth, that's all.

There's a lot of things I'd like different in the world. But I can't say I got so much to complain of. If I'd had more education like as not I'd be getting more pay. Maybe, I wouldn't. Not getting no schooling is my own fault. Poor or rich, humans is faulty one way or the next. Time I got to the seventh grade I got the making of money in my head. Wages looked to be about the best thing in the world. Well, I had a run of good jobs. Made fair money for a year or two driving trucks. Took a turn at auto fixing, too, around a filling station. Just first one thing and another. Jobs was easy to get then. That's before women got set on going to work. That's what caused all this depression business. I'm not saying that the women don't need jobs now. They does. But they got themselves to thank for the fix the world's in. They started out taking jobs from men when there wasn't no sense in them working. Them men lost out on good jobs and dropped right down and took ours. Just wasn't no jobs left for poor folks.

They Don't Know Nothing About Nothing

Folks that ain't never been poor just don't know nothin' a-tall about doing on nothing. I get so all-fired full of laugh when some of these women from the higher ups comes down to the Welfare Department. Nice ladies, but it ain't a salt spoon of sense about poor folks in their heads. Pretty little thing come last week to tell the women come here about cooking. Before she started spieling [talking], she seen them cans of salmon I took from the big case and put on that shelf back there. That give her a start. She aimed to tell them how to make up a pot dish from salmon. We ain't really got no salmon here. Just a cheap grade of canned mackerel. She sailed in. "Brush the baking dish with melted butter," says she. If she hadn't been so pretty and so young, I'd liked to asked right off—"Where they going to get the butter? Ain't two in the rooms got butter for their bread. You'll have to shift to a skillet for the cooking. That's about the best they

got for greasing up." Of course I didn't say no such to her.
She was just plumb wore out time she got that salmon out of
her head and into the cook stove. When she come to tail part
of the talk giving them leave to ask her questions, she looked
to me about ready to fall off the box I'd drug out for her to
speak from. It's a blessing the Lord made it easy for some.
A blessing. And I'm glad He done it.

My Wife and Kids

My wife's one ain't got no easy going. She do all the house
work. Washing. Ironing. Sewing. Cooking. There's eight of
us counting me and her. Six children. Me and Ella took a
marrying notion when we wasn't to no age. Without a penny laid by. Two that age ain't got no sense about what's to
come. Ella ain't never throwed in my face talk of things she
ought to have. Things I ain't been able to give her. She's
been poor all her life. She ain't got as much schooling as
me. No further than the fifth grade. Same year we's married
our first young one come along. They's come two years part
regular since then. All boys but the last one. We got the
sharpest little girl baby I ever seen. Born past July. Suits me
alright. I'm proud to have one like her. Girls mostly have a
hard time. Ought not have too many. Especially when
thing's like they's now. Me and the boys can take care of sister. I aim to see she gets a shot at schooling. I'd like to get
that little farm I'm set on while she's little. Give her just the
kind of playing and eating she ought to have.

Lord, there's one thing a man with a wife and kids got to
do—hang on to some sort of steady work. Get the most pay
he can. When we's first married, I was carrying freight all
over the state. Trucking for a big concern. I just throwed up
that job. Thought I'd pick up another one in no time. I'd just
got plumb sick of sleeping and eating in cheap boarding
places. Being away from Ella all the time. I just quit.

Well I wasn't as smart as I thought. I'd get first one thing
and next for piece time. No steady work. The depression come
on. I really wasn't trained to do much of nothing except drive
a car and do mechanics round filling stations. And in them two

lines looked like I couldn't find nothing. I said to Ella, "I ain't no fool and I ain't proud. I'm going to get something steady if it's digging ditches." Look like the Lord know'd I meant what I said. Next week I got wind of the janitor job over the City Welfare Department being open. They seen hard work wasn't no matter to me. I didn't ask one thing or another about all the things they aimed for the janitor to do. I just said, "I wants that job and I needs it." They give it to me. Driving the car for the Director was throwed in extra to the cleaning and such. And I was plumb glad it was. I come right up from that job to where I'm now. I'm in charge of supplies and keeping track of the stuff that comes in and is give out. I still drive the car for the Director. It ain't good for a man to spend most of his time in a hole damp and dark as this basement. Driving that car give me a shot at a little fresh air and sunshine. And I needs it.

Just goes to show the Lord'll work things out for us if we give him a chance. When I come down here I thought to myself—"Well, I'll put up with it till things takes turn for better." Why it's just drug us along through hard times! I get my transportation. Food supplies. Clothes. They leave me take the pick of them sent in for poor families. Take shoes— you just try to keep shoes on growing kids. See what a hole it knocks in your cash. I'm glad I'm in on the ground and gets the first drag at what's sent in. And working for the city I don't have to pay my own house rent. No that to me's about the best part of the job. Sickness come along like as not a man'll take rent money for doctoring and time comes to pay up he ain't put it back for rent like he thought he would. Out he and his goes. Unless he's got a mighty fine landlord. There's a few of that kind. Most is in the business for the money, though, and nothing else.

Ten Dollars a Week

Asides from groceries and rent and clothes there's ten dollars a week wages. I figger our spending, all told, about twenty dollars a month. Things we got to have that ain't give us is bought on the installment plan. Cost more that way. But what you going to do when things got to be got and there's no spot cash to hand! We's pulling long through debt right well. Just fifteen dollars owing on the furniture and about twenty-five on the washing machine. Lord, that washing machine's worth ever cent we paid for it. I told Ella if I ever seen another thing that'd be as big help to her I'd buy it if I had to bust a bank. It don't take her half the time used to to get all them youngun's clothes did and the house things and such. Ella keep everthing from the kids to the kivers clean as a pin. House the same. We keep our kids close to home. Don't let them run round with just any trash. I got the last one of ours insured for burial—except sister. I'll get her fixed time she's year old. I pay twenty cents a week on me and Ella. Ten cents for the two oldest boys, five cents for the others.

Thing that worries me most about a large family is the feeding of them right. I know ours don't have what they's supposed to. Not if half's right I hear them ladies who come here to talk says. We can't manage the milk we should for them. If we get Grade A they ain't enough for more than a cup around. I guess that cheap canned milk's good enough for cooking. We uses what they give us. Them things concocted for the place of butter ain't as cheap as you'd think. I ain't strong like I used to be. And with all this talk I hear floating round I wonder if its the things I ain't had to eat that'd done it.

I aim if we ever get out of debt to study about things like that. Give our kids ever fool thing folks says they ought to have to miss miseries that might take them off. I want to buy me about three acres of land. That'd be much as I could work. Build me a nice little house on it. I'd raise chickens, have a garden, two or three good cows and some pigs. I seen advertised in the paper where you could pick up acres of land round here cheap as ten dollars down and ten months coming till its paid for. How a man's going to live and bring up a big family on what the higher-ups call 'minimum wages' is something to study about. I tries to do the best I knows how. I guess the Lord don't ask more of nobody than that. But I'd be a lots easier in my head if I could get together enough to buy that little farm for me and Ella and the kids. A lots easier."

Hard Times in Harlem

Anna Arnold Hedgeman

During the Depression, urban black Americans not only experienced job discrimination they also had a hard time finding decent places to live. Many landlords would not rent to minorities at all. Landlords in Harlem, New York, took advantage of the situation by hiking up rent. To afford the exorbitant rent, multiple families moved in together into single family dwellings. In 1929, Anna Arnold Hedgeman worked for the YWCA. After the stock market crash, all the relief agencies, including the YWCA, were forced to bear a heavy burden. In this excerpt from her autobiography Hedgeman describes her experiences working in Harlem and what she saw as a social worker. Anna Arnold Hedgeman later went on to become an author, civil rights activist, and a politician who served in the New York City cabinet.

In Harlem I helped organize the unemployed, screened them for training, set up referral services to the Works Progress Administration (WPA) and National Youth Administration, established workshops for seamstresses, recruited nurses' aides for hospital duty, assisted in manning soup kitchens, and deployed street-corner apple salesmen. . . .

It was not until the depression that most members of our Harlem YWCA staff recognized that we had been dealing in services for people who could afford to pay. Except for our speeches in churches and civic organizations, we had

had limited contact with the masses of people. Even the churchgoers we knew had steady employment and they paid for mortgages, salaries and upkeep of their respective churches. In 1929 our agency and others like it discovered the rest of the community.

The New York State Temporary Commission report shows that in twenty-five years Harlem's population had increased more than 600 per cent to over 350,000 (equal to the total population of Rochester, N.Y.), with an average density of 233 persons per acre compared with 133 for the rest of Manhattan. The community had become a vast swarming hive in which families were doubled and trebled in inadequate apartments. With the financial collapse in October 1929, a large mass of Negroes were faced with the reality of starvation and they turned sadly to public relief. A few chanted optimistically, "Jesus will lead me and the Welfare will feed me," but others said it was a delusion, for the Home Relief Bureau allowed only eight cents a meal for food. Meanwhile men, women and children combed the streets and searched in garbage cans for food, foraging with dogs and cats.

Low Quality of Life

The crashing drop of wages drove Negroes back to the already crowded hovels east of Lenox Avenue. In many blocks one toilet served a floor of four apartments. Most of the apartments had no private bathrooms or even the luxury of a public bath. Where a tub could be found, it usually had been installed in the kitchen. All of these tenements were filthy and vermin-ridden. There were flats with old-fashioned toilets which rarely flushed, and when they did, overflowed on the floors below. In the winter, gaping holes in the skylights allowed cold air to sweep down the staircase. Coal grates provided the only heat. The tenants scoured the neighborhood for fuel, and harassed janitors in the surrounding districts were compelled to stand guard over coal deliveries until they were safely stored in the cellars. Landlords in this section hired a janitor for nothing more than a basement room, for which he had to clean six floors, take care of side-walks and backyard, haul garbage, make minor repairs, and, where there was one, stoke the hot-water furnace.

Many families had been reduced to living below street level. It was estimated that more than ten thousand Negroes lived in cellars and basements which had been converted into makeshift flats. Packed in damp, rat-ridden dungeons, they existed in squalor not too different from that of the Arkansas sharecroppers. Floors were of cracked concrete, and the walls were whitewashed rock, water-drenched and rust-streaked. There were only slits for a window and a tin can in a corner was the only toilet.

Shunted into these run-down sections, Negroes were forced to pay exorbitant rents to landlords who flagrantly violated the city building and sanitary codes. Compared with the 20 to 25 per cent of their income white families generally paid for rent, Negro tenants paid from 40 to 50 per cent. More than half the Negro families were forced to take in lodgers to augment the family income. Frequently whole families slept in one room. Envied was the family who had a night worker as a lodger, for he would occupy a bed in the day that would be rented out at night—same room, same bed, same sheets and same bedbugs. This was described as the "hot bed." If the family had a bathtub, it too, was covered with boards, and rented out.

Not Enough Aid to Go Around

Most social agencies set up special funds to meet the emergency needs of those who came to the organization. We had to visit the homes of such people, for our funds were limited and we tried to give our aid to the worst emergencies. Most of us had had no experience with need at this elemental level and everything looked like an extreme emergency. I found myself making decisions on the basis of the number of children immediately in need of milk. I learned to fight evictions, to secure the suspension of rent claims, to suggest employment possibilities where that was possible.

Here again I came into contact with mass employment

discrimination. Interestingly enough the trade union movement and the public utilities were the major offenders.

The dress trades would not hire Negroes ostensibly because they were not union members and the union would not accept them because there was no work open to them. Finally, the desperate farm situation of the South brought an increased number of Negro sharecroppers into Harlem.

The Negro churches played an heroic role as did the neighbors of people who were suffering. As social workers we were faced with the necessity of continuously making long-range plans and at the same time feeding and sheltering as many young people as our funds would support.

Chapter 3

Making a Buck

Chapter Preface

With unemployment so high and jobs so scarce during the 1930s, people tended to hold onto whatever work they could get. Oftentimes the only thing available were odd jobs painting, cleaning, or picking fruit. Many employers took advantage of the depressed market by increasing hours and dropping wages. Both employer and employee knew there was always somebody willing to work for less. The mine owners in the coal industry exploited this sobering reality. Historically, miners had always endured hardship, but during the Depression the conditions in the coal mines of such states as Kentucky were inhuman.

The people who couldn't find regular jobs resorted to the many get-rich-quick schemes that seemed to flourish during the thirties. Marathon dancing and flagpole sitting were two ways to get into the record books and possibly earn a little money. There were fees and disqualifications that weren't apparent if one didn't carefully read the contract. In fact, the only people who were assured any fortune were the promoters who came up with the schemes. But at least it was a diversion from the day-to-day drudgery of looking for work.

Of course the fun was short-lived and certainly not pervasive. A lot of blood was spilled in fierce battles between labor and business in many industries. Some of the strikes became armed conflicts that resulted in deaths on both sides. John L. Lewis, leader of the United Mine Workers, was one of the most prominent labor leaders during the era. Lewis's tireless lobbying efforts were responsible for many of the labor laws that allowed the worker to safely organize, protest, and renegotiate wages. But it would be a long battle that would force employers to accept that the relationship between worker and business and business and government would be a lot different from then on.

Passing the Time on Your Feet

June Havoc

More than any other commodity, people during the Depression had a lot of idle time. Jobs were scarce and waiting for something to happen could be disheartening, so people participated in a multitude of silly activities in an attempt to get rich or famous or simply pass the time. Flagpole and tree sitting, six-day bicycle races, and marathon dancing were just a few of the many preoccupations that possessed the idle in the thirties.

The following excerpt is from actress June Havoc's biography and describes her early years on the marathon dance circuit. Marathon dances were contests of stamina that required a couple to be the last dancers on their feet at the end of the time allotted. To make things interesting, marathon promoters would throw in a "sprint" every few hours in which the exhausted couples were expected to literally run around the dance arena. Sprints were good for livening up the entertainment as well as thinning out the competition. The marathon often dragged on for weeks and even months. The longer the contest lasted the more money the promoter made from ticket admission. The prize money advertised was large, but after all the fees the promoter charged the contestants for laundry and food and other incidentals, the promoter was often the only one who made any real money.

M r. Burke's whistle brought me back to the present. My focus wasn't very sharp, but I knew Patsy and I were once again the lead-off team. We were lined up and ready to sprint. Mr. Burke was walking to the center of the dance floor like a circus ringmaster. If more color was what the audience wanted, they were going to be obliged, because on this start-off Mr. Burke was employing a little extra drama. Over his head he held a very fat revolver. First he squeezed his eyes shut and then the trigger.

The blank cartridge made a terrible sound as we catapulted into the race. Shot out of a cannon, I thought grimly as Patsy and I careened around the posts. . . . The race was on once again. Time hung suspended. There was no Time; it was just Now.

Pent-up Emotions and Exhausted Bodies

I don't know how much later I became aware of a bubbling sound behind me. It grew into a soft chuckle. From there it developed into a sobbing, humorless giggle, and then burst into wild, maniacal, tearing laughter. Patsy and I got a glimpse of Bozo's red, puffing features.

Helen was shaking his hands as they hurtled around the corners wildly, trying to push him back into reality. He plodded along, his big mouth wide open. Mr. Burke turned in the center of the floor, following Bozo's galloping, hysterical figure. It was clear that Mr. Burke wasn't certain about laughter being a penalty. He was trying to make up his mind. The crowd sensed this and immediately took sides. Helen redoubled her efforts to control Bozo's wild, sobbing laughter. She banged his face with the side of her head.

"Throw him out!" some of the voices screamed.

"No fair! No fair!" shouted the others.

Ruddy [a judge] joined Mr. Burke in the center of the ring as we thumped around them. He gestured that he didn't consider a laugh a spoken word. Mr. Burke shook his head. He thought it was. The crowd yelled.

Helen hoped the argument would occupy the two men in the center of the floor, so she broke contact with Bozo long enough to hit him violently across the face, then quickly grabbed his hand again. The crowd's voice rose to a shattering shriek at the gesture.

Mr. Burke and Ruddy whirled about, confused. They knew they had missed something.

Mr. Burke sidestepped through the posts to get a penalty card to pin on Bozo. He held up the little oilcloth square and started back toward the center of the arena. Suddenly Helen's wiry, hard little body flew at him. She left Bozo, who stupidly galloped about the posts alone, taking the turns neatly and sobbing a little more quietly. Her fists pounded into Mr. Burke's expensive clothing. Her voice rose in a furious screech.

"No! No! Leave him alone! You touch him and I'll—I'll kill you. Kill you! I'll kill you!"

I watched Bozo's bobbing figure. He wiped his nose like a little boy, blinked his eyes and gulped. But he never missed a beat.

"Hold That Tiger!" the band played.

"Kill him! Kill him! Beat him up, Helen!" the crowd roared.

Ruddy tried to grab Helen's flailing arms. She turned on him, kicking out with her feet. She screamed, "Don't touch me! Get away from me! All of you!"

They closed in on her. She was carried off the floor, arms and legs flying, hoarsely screaming, "I'll kill you! I'll kill you!"

We were left thumping and panting around the floor to the wild music.

Mr. Burke reappeared somewhat disheveled, holding a handkerchief to his right eye. He blew his whistle: Toot! Toot! Toot! Toot! Toot! The music wheezed to a stop. We clung to one another, trembling and wet.

"Ladies and gentlemen, quiet, please!" Ruddy shouted. "Come here, Bozo. Ladies and gentlemen," Ruddy began in his best funereal tones, "what you have just witnessed is the result of the pent-up emotions and exhausted bodies of these brave kids."

A trainer carried Helen center-stage. The orchestra began the soft, nostalgic "My Buddy." . . . The big trainer held Helen's tiny figure easily.

Ruddy went into his spiel: "They're out of the money,

Marathon dances were not only a grueling test of stamina, they were also a way for people to pass the time during the Depression.

ladies and gentlemen. All these hours have gone for nothing for poor little Helen unless you reach into your pockets and make this shower truly a silver shower!"

Bozo's voice interrupted the dramatic moment: "What's the matter with her?" he asked in a businesslike tone. His eyes had cleared and he'd come out of his squirrely stage.

"Sshh!" Ruddy admonished. "Do you want to louse it up for yourself?" Ruddy cleared his throat. "Twenty-four hours—that's all Bozo has as solo. If one of the boy dancers drops out, Bozo will have a chance at the leftover girl and the prize money. If not, ladies and gentlemen,

Bozo's long hours will be wasted."

The silver shower was all anybody could ask for. Ruddy kept a firm grip on the big man beside him, and in a little while we were back to the regular routine. Patsy was elected to tell Bozo the bad news. "He didn't say anything—he just cried." Patsy's report to us was a flat statement. There was no comment.

Eating and Sleeping on Your Feet

The twelve-o'clock meal found us emerging from the rest quarters clad for the night in trousers, sweaters and comfortable shoes. We weaved alongside the rocking-horse table. All of us eyed Bozo. Each girl must have had her own separate thoughts. Bozo was a lug—a dangerous lug. Heavy, clumsy, he staggered and threw himself about in his sleep. Only Helen could possibly carry him. The night facing us would see Bozo alone. His eyes dropped now as he fought off sleep. Tonight he would be a lonely lug.

I looked at Patsy. He was watching the red-faced man, too.

"You want to sleep now?" I asked.

"Next period," he answered. "And, remember, stay out of Bozo's way tonight. We only got one more fall for me.[1] If I'm out you fall heir to Two Ton. You don't want to carry that big lug, do you?"

I looked over at Bozo. He had lifted a large spoonful of soup to his mouth, his eyes half closed. The soup spilled down his chin. He was asleep.

"No," I said quietly. "Oh, no. Patsy, who besides Mr. Dankle dreams up things like—well, sprints, grinds, and using those awful red and blue lights?"

Patsy looked at the Christmas tree lights still blinking along the ropes. "I dunno," he said. "The same guys that dream up Mother's Day, I guess—and the Easter Bunny. You know, guys with a real load of sentiment and all that crap."

That night points and falls already acquired would remain

---

1. A contestant was eliminated from the competition if he or she fell—usually while asleep—a certain number of times.

fixed. However, we could talk to each other and we could break contact. We could go to the bathroom, if necessary. This was to be a luxurious night. The three-o'clock meal saw us gathered at the same table, but this time Patsy was asleep. I had tied his hands with a handkerchief and lowered his arms over my head so that his long frame rested its weight on my back.

I drank my coffee slowly. The Schwartzes both thought they were eating, but they wobbled against the table, half in and half out of consciousness. Jewel's face lay flat in her bread and butter. The others were silently shuffling around the floor. The night matron was up front having coffee with the trainer and Mr. James, the night judge. Three or four drunks slept it off around the ringside. Up in the bleachers two couples were in intimate conversation as they passed around a bottle of gin.

After All That Effort

A small, hollow-eyed figure appeared in the entrance to the girls' quarters. It was Helen. A limp terry-cloth robe hung on her skinny shoulders. Her swollen, callused feet were bare. She walked silently around to the second box [ringside seating area] and picked her way to the front chair.

"Baby," she whispered. "Baby come over here." Bozo's staggering form stopped. His back was toward her. He was facing us. His eyes opened partly. "Come over here, baby. Come on, now!" Helen's voice was soft and caressing. Bozo's florid face relaxed into a childishly happy smile. He lifted his head and turned.

"Here I am," Helen cooed, "over here. That's right. Come on, now." Unsteadily, Bozo sensed the direction and began shuffling toward her. She held her arms up to him. "That's my boy. That's my big baby. Come on, now." He had almost reached her outstretched arms. "Don't fall," she cautioned gently. "Don't fall down, baby." She took his hands and lifted herself up onto the floor. Crawling over the railing, she patted his face and gently put his huge head on her shoulder.

"Now," she murmured to him, "you see? Everything's going to be all right." He was bent almost double, his weight relaxed as Helen's back stiffened.

It was all so very quiet. The unsuspecting night crew could be heard enjoying themselves over their coffee. Helen slowly backed off the floor, rocking Bozo from one foot to the other. She sang softly. It was a nursery tune with silly words: "This little piggy went to market, this little piggy stayed home, this little piggy had roast beef, this little piggy would roam. . . ."

Her voice fell to an almost imperceptible humming sound as she disappeared from our view, gently dragging Bozo in her wake.

I hiked Patsy's frame to a more comfortable position across my shoulders and started circling the floor. A few minutes later there was a sudden silence in the direction of the coffee bar. Mr. James hurried up the aisle between the bleachers. The trainer swiftly began searching the floor of each box left of us, while the night matron did the same on the right side. They had a hurried consultation. The men disappeared into the rest quarters.

"Where's Bozo?" the matron asked.

"He went to bed," I replied. "Helen came out and took him to bed." The trainer returned, an amused smile on his face. "I'll be damned," he said. "She's in there rocking and singing away, and that big hunk of beef is sound asleep in her arms, happy as a puppy!"

The Work Was Never Steady

Henry Boucher

Everybody seemed to prosper during the postwar years. The economy was growing rapidly, investors were making a fortune in the stock market, and new technologies were creating new jobs. Experienced tradesmen could always find work someplace when the economy was good. But when the Depression hit and demand for goods plummeted it became difficult for even the most skilled workers to stay employed for very long. Henry Boucher had been a textile worker for many years. He had established a good reputation. During the hard times many of the mills were downsizing or closing, forcing Henry and his family to live on his savings. His account was recorded by a Mr. Guilfoyle of the Works Progress Administration (WPA) in 1939.

Editors Note: The following text is taken from the WPA record of oral and written testimony of Depression victims. In retyping the information, some original words from the text have been lost. The editors of the record have inserted possible reconstructions of lost text in brackets. The text within these insertions is emended with a question mark to denote its hypothetical nature.

In 1928 work in the mills began to slacken and I was laid off. After being [out?] of work for two months I secured employment in the Saranac mill [in Northeastern New York] as a weaver. At this job I received $40 a week, but I believed that in a short time I would again find employment as warp-

Excerpted from Henry Boucher's account before the Works Progress Administration, 1939.

starter. The next year conditions were worse and I was without work for three months. My wife and I were not worried about the future, as we believed that the mills would be slack for only a short period, as they were in 1921. So we lived on what I made and did not touch the $3,500 that we had in the bank. I was without work for six months in 1930 and we were forced to use some of the money that we had saved. But I was in a better position than most of my friends who were buying houses and were unable to meet their payments. My brother Peter was caught in this condition and as the bank was going to foreclose on his house I loaned him $500. I knew that he, a cutter in the rubber shop, making $70 a week, would be able to repay me as soon as his work picked up. Then, without warning, the rubber shop closed down and moved out of the city, throwing 1,500 people out of work. The next year, 1931, the bottom dropped out of everything and we were forced to use up most of our savings. In only one way, was I fortunate, and that was that I had no more doctor's bills to pay, as my wife was well again. The bank foreclosed on my brother's house and my $500 was gone. My father died in July and after the funeral my mother came to live with me. She did not live long after my father but died in October, 1931. As neither my father nor mother believed in life insurance, all of their children contributed to the cost of the funerals. I was unable to find work and spent the entire year hanging around the streets. By the end of 1931 my bank balance was less than $500 and going down rapidly.

In September, 1932 I reached the end of my resources. I was desperate, with a wife and three children to support I was unable to find work of any kind. All of my friends were in the same predicament. Finally I had to go on relief, and what a relief that was! I shall always remember my experience while trying to get relief from the city. I went down to City Hall and registered at the Poor Department. After looking me up they gave me a pass to obtain food. But in order to receive the food I had to stand in line on Main Street with every passerby staring at me.

One day I stood in a line that blocked one side of Main Street for four hours before I received a small bag of flour and two pounds of dried peas. Of course my family was unable to live on what I received from the Poor Department so I was continually moving to cheaper tenements until at last I was living in a basement on Social Street. The same type of tenement that I was born in. The home that I had taken such pride in was broken up and the fine furniture that my wife and I had worked for we had to sell to second-hand furniture dealers. It is not correct to say that I sold the furniture because the money that I received for it was so little that it was almost equivalent to giving it away. But my children had to have food and clothing. The rent had to be paid and coal to be bought.

There was a soup kitchen on Social Street and my son would go down there with a pail and bring home some soup. This helped out the small amount of food that I received from the Poor Department and kept my family from actual starvation. My family was very poor when I was a child and when work in the mills was slack we would not have much to eat, but in Woonsocket never before was it necessary for anyone to have to go to a public soup kitchen in order not to starve.

Lucky to Get Half

In 1934 I obtained employment as a weaver in the Montrose mill. I worked steady the whole year except for a few weeks when the mill was closed by a strike. But working conditions had changed. They were as different as day and night from the working conditions of the 1920 to 1930 period. The pay had been greatly reduced and the amount of work per man had been increased. I had been making $40 a week as a weaver operating two looms. Now I am operating six looms on the same material and only making $24 a week. I am lucky that I am working on fine worsted cloth because in some mills on coarser cloth, the weavers now operate from eight to twenty-four looms for $24 a week. Apparently the only thing that a textile worker can rely upon in these times is that the mill owner will never suffer lower profits as long as he can transfer the burden upon his employees.

In 1935 I was again laid off and the money that I had made in 1934 was soon used up, then back to the relief I went. Since that time I have worked about six months in each year, and being unable to support my family when I am not working, I usually spend the rest of the year on the relief. The last place that I worked was in the Montrose as a weaver, in the Spring of 1938. I worked here for four months but I knew that it would not last forever.

One morning I left my house and as I entered the weave shop I could sense the tension that seemed to be in the air. The looms clattered, the men moved about. The belts and pulleys whirred. A typical weave room interior. But on this

A Day's Work Here and a Day's Work There

Long-term, regular employment was scarce during the Depression. Most people who were employed held onto their jobs as long as possible, even after pay cuts and increases in working hours. Many of the unemployed survived by taking on any odd jobs they could find. The following excerpt is from Robert J. Hastings autobiography, A Nickel's Worth of Skim Milk, *in which Hastings recalls his father's various employment during the 1930s.*

The closing of Old West Side Mine meant the end of anything resembling a steady job for the next eight years. From 1930 on, it was a day's work here and a day's work there, a coal order from the welfare office, a relief check, a few days on WPA [Works Progress Administration], a garden in the back yard, and a few chickens and eggs.

We weathered the storm because of Dad's willingness to take any job and Mom's ability to stretch every available dollar. It was not so much a matter of finding a job as of filling in with odd jobs wherever and whenever you could, and most of the "jobs" were those you made for yourself.

My diary shows that Dad sold iron cords door to door,

Friday morning there was something lacking. No one was talking, there was no laughter. Joseph Boyce, who worked next to me, did not raise his head from his work to call a greeting, nor did he ask me how I intended to spend the weekend, as he was wont to do. Everyone was silently working, busy with their thoughts. For about a week past there had been rumors that the work in the mill was getting slack. Only three days ago six spinners were laid off and the rumor was that eight weavers would lose their jobs this afternoon. I was, in length of service, one of the youngest weavers in the mill and I believed that I would be one of the first to be laid off. But there was nothing sure about it. Sometimes an old hand, whom the boss disliked was laid off

---

"worked a day in the hay," bought a horse to break gardens, rented an extra lot for a garden on the shares, picked peaches, raised sweet potato slips, traded an occasional dozen of eggs at the grocery, hung wallpaper, "painted Don Albright's house for $5," picked up a day or two's work at the strip mines, guarded the fence at the county fairgrounds, cut hair for boys in the neighborhood, sold coal orders, and when he had to and could, worked intermittently on WPA.

With no dependable income, we cut back on everything possible. We stopped the evening paper, turned off the city water and cleaned out our well, sold our four-door Model T touring car with the snap-on side curtains and isinglass, stopped ice and milk delivery, and disconnected our gas range for all but the three hot summer months. There was no telephone to disconnect, as we didn't have one to start with!

We did keep up regular payments on two Metropolitan Life Insurance policies. Page after page of old receipt books show entries of 10¢ per week on one policy and 69¢ a month on another. As long as we could, we made house payments to the Marion Building and Loan, but a day came when we had to let those go, too.

Robert J. Hastings, *A Nickel's Worth of Skim Milk: A Boy's View of the Great Depression.* Carbondale, IL: Southern Illinois University Press, 1972.

and a newcomer kept. This uncertainty kept every weaver under a strain until they knew just who was to get the bounce. So they continued to work hard and silently until lunch time, for this was one day that no one wanted to make a mistake and have the foreman's attention called to him. While eating lunch the weavers could talk of nothing but who was to be laid off. While the newcomers believed that they would be the first to go, many of the old-timers remembered how they had spoiled yards of cloth and how displeased the boss had been with them. They wondered if he would remember the many times that he had bawled them out and take revenge by letting them go. So in this frame of mind the weavers started the afternoon shift.

This afternoon the foreman of the weave room did not walk around the room as he was accustomed to do, and it was nearly the close of the afternoon before he stepped from his office. Instantly, the eyes of all the weavers were upon him, watching where he was going, and each man hoping that the foreman would not come to him with the sad news. I saw the foreman turn to a weaver and start talking to him. They talked for a few minutes while everyone in the room watched. The foreman then turned away and approached another weaver. The first weaver spread his arms out wide in a gesture and everyone then knew that the foreman was laying off help. All eyes then turned to the foreman, watching to see who was being laid off. I watched the slow progress of the foreman as he went from man to man, telling them the bad news. He was now at the next loom and I prayed that I might be spared. But it was not to be, for the foreman slowly walked over to me and said, "You know what I have to say. I have a list of men who are to be laid off and your name is on it. They are laying off in every room of the mill and if more work don't come in the rest of the weavers will be out next week. This is no reflection upon your work, which has been good; and I'll be glad to hire you back just as soon as the work picks up." I replied, "Well, I guess all the fellows here are in the same boat that I'm in. All of us are broke. This will mean plenty of hardship for my family.

After eating good for the past five months, the first few meals of that relief canned corn beef is going to be hell for the kids. But thanks for your offer to rehire me when the work picks up. I'll certainly be glad too to get back to work." The foreman then returned to his office and the weavers gathered into a group asking each other what the boss said to them. The men who were laid off now that the tension had been broken, began to joke and one said, "Will Johnny Ryan, the Director of Public Aid be glad to see me? Like hell he will. The last time I was on relief I had to haunt him in order to get any commodities. Every time he turned around I would be at his elbow asking for something." Another said, "This loafing is all right in some ways but I'll always blame the last lay off for the twins my wife had." I said, "I wonder how long I'll have to wait for my unemployment compensation checks. The last time I had to wait ten weeks before I got the first one and then the amount was wrong." And so for a few minutes they joked and talked of the future. They then returned to work.

The Same Old Thing

My mind was not on my looms. I was thinking of the greatly lowered standard of living that my family would have to endure while I was out of work. I thought of my new radio that I was paying one dollar a week on. That would soon be taken back by the dealer. And then there was the dreadful ordeal of informing my wife and children that I had been laid off. I knew that there would be no happiness or laughter in my home this night. How could I support my family on the six or seven dollars a week that I would receive from a relief? How long would I be without work this time? I stood there thinking these gloomy thoughts, not caring how my looms ran. What did I care now if a "smash" or dropped thread was made in the cloth? Let some one else worry about that. At bell time I made a bundle of my overalls and silently slipped out of the mill. I started walking home wishing that the road was twice as long so that I would not have to face my family so soon.

When I reached home my wife saw by the sorrowful look upon my face that something had gone wrong and she asked, "What is the matter Henry?" I replied, "The same old thing. I'm laid off and don't know when I'll go back." Across my wife's face an expression of fear flashed but she quickly rallied and said. "Well, you can't help that, so stop looking as though you were at your own wake. We have been on relief before and we're still alive so sit down and eat your supper. You'll feel better then." I sat down at the table but could eat very little. All this time the children, seated around the table, had been listening to the conversation and looking at me with wide staring eyes. Only too well did they know what this meant, less food, no new clothes, no money to go to the movies, peeking through the window curtains when someone knocked upon the door, to see if it was a bill collector, moving to a less desirable tenement in short, misery for everyone in the family. After supper I was unable to stand the silence and gloom that seemed to settle over the house so I put on my coat and said, "Alice, I'm going down to the corner for a minute." My wife, knowing full well where I was going said, "Make sure you come home sober." So, leaving the house I hurriedly walked to "Fat's" saloon. In there, men would be talking upon every subject. There would also be jokes and laughter and for a few hours I could forget that my next pay would be the last one that I would receive for a long time.

The next day I applied for my unemployment compensation and because of waiting for these cheeks I was unable to go on the relief for two months. By this time I was completely broke, so for the next few months we struggled along on the six dollars a week that I received from the relief. But week by week we were going deeper in debt for rent, electricity, and many other small bills. One morning a deputy sheriff handed me an eviction notice and departed. And there I sat, in the kitchen, alone, forlorn and in despair. It was the morning of November 25, just one month before Christmas, and in my hand I held the notice from the court to evacuate the tenement that I occupied. This was not the first eviction notice that I had ever received. During the past ten years, the deputy sheriffs had worn a path to my door delivering eviction notices, writs of attachment and liens on my pay. How could I break the news to my wife, when she returned from a visit to a neighbor's house? Where could we go? When you are on relief and only receive six dollars a week it is impossible to support a family and pay rent. The landlords did not care to rent a tenement to families on relief as they could not be sure of their rent. So most of them were demanding their rent in advance. If I could find a tenement, where could I borrow the three dollars for the first week's rent? What a Christmas was in store for my children! As I sat there alone with my thoughts the door opened and my wife walked in. Without talking I handed her the eviction notice. She knew what it was. She had seen many of them since 1930. Silently she laid it down and started to prepare dinner, each of us wondering where we could find a tenement.

Good News

A knock on the door. We looked at each other. What more trouble was coming to us? Good news had been absent from our lives for more than ten years. My wife slowly and listlessly walked to the door and opened it.

There stood Adrian Bonin, with a broad smile upon his face and he said, "O boy, Henry, I have thees fine news for you. De boss wants for you to come to work tomorrow morning. Thees mill she's get the big order. We'll work all winter." It seemed like a miracle, the house seemed brighter, wide smiles appeared upon our faces. We started asking questions of Adrian. Who was the order for? What looms would I have? How does the yarn run? Which of the men were going back to work? Adrian answered as best he could and soon left. Dinner was forgotten and my wife and I were still talking in an excitable manner when our children came in for dinner. They sensed the jovial mood of my wife and myself and when they heard the news they too forgot about dinner in thinking of the happiness that this news meant. Their father was going back to work. There would be new clothes for all and toys and presents at Christmas. After the children had gone to bed Alice and I sat up talking. We planned how we would spend my first week's pay to the best advantage. By paying a little each week on the old bills we would soon be out of debt. We would not have to move now for as soon as the landlord knew that I was working he would forget about his eviction notice. And if we needed money at Christmas we could easily borrow it from the small loan company. So in a happy frame of mind we went to bed.

The next morning I was at the mill gates an hour before bell time. There I found all of my fellow workers and I joined in their conversation. Each asked the other what they had been doing during the lay off and what were they going to do with their first pay? There were predictions, laughingly made that "Fat's" saloon would do a rushing business on pay night. But under all this gay jesting everyone of us knew that when the order was finished in a few months, we would again be laid off, to tramp the streets while we collected our unemployment compensation checks and then back on relief we would have to go until the mill started running full time again. We had gone through this routine many times in the past ten years and each one of us knew that he would go through it many times in the future. But that knowledge could not dim our spirits today because we knew that while the mill operated we would be able to eat what we wanted, we could dress our families and have a dollar left so that when meeting our fellow workers in "Fat's" saloon on Saturday night each one of us could stand up to the bar and pay for a round of beers.

An Artist in Hard Times

Frank W. Long

Like any other craftsmen during the Depression, fine artists of all talents had difficult times supporting themselves solely with their skills. The demand for art was very low and job prospects were limited. Frank W. Long was an artist in Illinois who took on many different kinds of day jobs. Working as a cake decorator and a busboy kept him afloat and gave him time to paint on his own. On occasion Long would be commissioned by a rich patron to paint, but in most cases it was a struggle to keep food on the table. Long eventually became a well-known mural painter for the WPA (Works Progress Administration). The WPA was one of President Roosevelt's New Deal Agencies that employed artists in many different capacities including creating sculpture, graphic design, and murals. Long's post office and library murals still exist today.

W hen I returned to the States from Europe early in 1929, the Great Depression was just getting under way. It was the worst possible time for an artist to think of trying to start a career. In Chicago, during the few months before the stock market crash, I managed to exist by several expedients. I found some work designing the icing decorations for wedding, birthday, and other special cakes, which were then executed by a caterer's pastry chefs; I also worked for an hour and a half each day as a busboy in a cafeteria in return for my meals. In addition, my ever-supportive parents came to my assistance during the leanest periods, although I knew they could hardly afford it.

In spite of the struggle, I managed somehow to continue painting during these hard times, and at last the tide seemed to turn. Another artist, a friend, introduced me to the director of the Walden-Dudensing Gallery, which had opened a short time before in the Drake Hotel on the lakeshore, a rather swanky setting. He came to my studio to see my work and was obviously impressed with what he saw. He offered me a one-man show for a couple of months in the spring of 1931. I was both surprised and elated. I spent every available hour on new work I hoped to have ready to exhibit, and I considered the result a good representation of my ability. The show looked very good when hung. The director, Mr. Manning, was very pleased with it and had a well-designed catalog printed. This was my first public exposure of any kind. Unfortunately, but no doubt predictably, not a single work was sold, not even a drawing! At the time, I considered this at least a minor tragedy.

Of course my failure could hardly have had anything to do with Mr. Dudensing's suicide a short time later. That was a result of the Wall Street crash, and his means of escape was one that became popular among previously wealthy businessmen at that time. The failure of the stock market also ushered in a period of desperation for many others who were barely making a living before it occurred, but being inured to financial hardship, few in that class resorted to self-destruction as a solution. For me, just as it seemed I had hit rock-bottom, Mr. Curt Teich appeared. Unknown to me, he was the owner of Curt Teich Lithograph Company, then the largest producer of colored picture postcards in the country.

A New Job Rolls In

As I remember it, it was on a bleak morning in October while I was gazing rather disconsolately out of my studio window that a long black chauffeured limousine came into view and pulled up to the curb across the street. This was on

Rush Street in what was called Towertown—Chicago's equivalent of New York's Greenwich Village, a haven of artists, musicians, poets, art students, dilettantes, impostors, would-be artists, and assorted hangers-on. It was given that name because it was a neighborhood of several streets near the old Water Tower on Michigan Boulevard in Chicago's "near north side." I lived there in a large rented room and bath that served as a studio for both myself and Vincent Ripley, a friend from my student days at the Art Institute. The long black car with chauffeur was not unusual in this neighborhood where there were several excellent restaurants and more than one speakeasy [illegal drinking establishments] (Prohibition was then in force), but when a portly middle-aged man got out, looked at the house numbers, and came directly across the street, I was curious. I entered the below-street-level vestibule of my building; after a moment, to my surprise, my bell rang. When I answered, a voice with a heavy German accent identified Curt Teich. He said he would like to talk with me about something he thought I might be interested in. With considerable wonder, I invited him to come up and unlocked the vestibule door.

When he was comfortably seated he began by introducing himself and saying he had recently been in Lexington, Kentucky, where he was introduced to my father, also a painter, by a friend of his who lived in that city. He said he had had the pleasure of visiting my parents in their home and had seen there a portrait of my father, painted by me. He professed great admiration for the picture, particularly the style in which it was done, coupled with the fact that he thought it a remarkable likeness. He said, in his thick German syllables, "Meester Long, I dell you vhy I am goming to zee you. I haf been dinking mebby I can get you to baint un bortrait of mine vife the zame vay you binted your fodder—zo beautiful mit ze liddle spots of color all over."

I had painted the portrait of my father when I was home on vacation from the Pennsylvania Academy of Fine Art in Philadelphia. We had been studying the impressionist and pointillist techniques of the French masters, and the painting had come off fairly well as a demonstration of painting with spots of pure primary and secondary colors placed side by side to create shades of tertiary and quaternary hues when viewed at a distance. This produced a vibration of the colors by mixing their optical images rather than the pigments themselves. I was surprised that this innovative technique would impress someone who I suspected was not familiar with its origin. He went on, "Of gourse I know you haf not zeen mine vife and you don't know vedder you like ze job or no. Zo I zink maby you like to gome mit me to spend ze veekend by mine home in Glengoe [Glenco, Illinois] and look her over before you mage up your mind. I minezelf zink she's looging bretty good, but you might be zinking uddervise." (The last was said with a little self-deprecating smile.)

Divine Intervention

I was utterly astonished and overwhelmed by the sudden decision of fate to smile on me in my economically precarious situation. A confirmed disbeliever in divine intervention in human affairs, I could not help thinking that, had I not been, I would have been unable to think of anything in either my behavior or my character that could have justified such salvation. Besides, I was genuinely puzzled that anyone would want so earnestly to have an unknown artist paint a picture of his wife, on what I thought was the questionable evidence of competence revealed in that painting of my father. Of course I could not confide these thoughts to Mr. Teich—I could only stammer my thanks for his appreciation of my work, and for his kind invitation. So it was arranged that he and his chauffeur would pick me up on Friday on their way from his plant on the south side to the north shore village, some forty miles from Chicago, where I was to spend the weekend "looging over" Madame Teich.

Of course I took "ze job." She was a very handsome and personable woman, decidedly paintable; and although I could not consider myself a portrait painter, I approached this commission with some anticipation of success. She was large, a good many pounds overweight, but with a figure that was definitely voluptuous. In the painting she was to be seated—it would be a three-quarter-length pose. I was sure I would enjoy doing it. Besides, I genuinely liked the subject, her husband, and their two children, a boy and a girl, both young teenagers. They were all interested in the progress of the portrait but agreed not to ask to see it until I should consider it finished. It was always a pleasure to spend the time that the sittings required with this gracious family in their home on the shore of the lake. It became routine that I would be picked up on Fridays and on other appointed days travel out by myself on the Skokie Valley Electric Train. The sittings, which usually lasted about two hours each, sometimes mornings, sometimes afternoons, took place in an upstairs sitting room in the Teich mansion where there was good north light from a large window.

Always Well Fed

One of the most attractive features of this unusual commission was an unstated emolument in the arrangement that kept me relatively well fed. In the course of the sittings it developed that I would normally share the Teich table on weekends and, more often than not, during the weekday sittings as well. In addition to this bountiful hospitality, I was usually offered a return-trip ticket for the train to Chicago. This thoughtfulness was characteristic of the Teichs and an indication that they fully realized my financial condition. Furthermore, to make it appear that this was not really charity, they would explain that the tickets were quite cheap when bought by the book.

Such liberality made me sometimes wonder if this concern for my welfare might have influenced the commission of the portrait as well; that is, if someone in the background might have sponsored the idea on my behalf, knowing that I needed the work. Of course this was a pretty far-fetched idea. There seemed to be no connection with anyone my family knew and the friend of Mr. Teich's who had introduced my father as a portrait painter simply by his reputation because his friend was looking for an artist to paint his wife's portrait. Then it occurred to me that I had possibly thwarted a commission that might have been intended for my dad. But this idea also seemed to belong in the realm of fantasy. And I knew that he would have renounced any interest in such a commission if he thought he could influence Teich to give me the job. If any of my imaginings did happen to be true, of course, my father would never have let me know it.

Pennies from Heaven

As pleasant and fortuitous as the conditions connected with the portrait were, there were some disruptions and setbacks too. The most memorable occurred one morning in December when I reported to the house to keep an appointment for a sitting at ten. I had walked the half mile from the train station in four inches of snow with leaky shoes. The maid who answered the doorbell was startled to see me.

"Why, Mr. Long!" she said. "Didn't Mrs. Teich reach you this morning? I know she was calling you early this morning to tell you she had been called into Chicago for an important meeting and would not be able to pose today." Evidently she hadn't got the message to my landlady before I left, or that sometimes-unreliable woman had failed to relay it to me.

Employed by the WPA (Works Progress Administration), Frank W. Long created murals such as this one during the Depression.

Although most inconvenient, the situation would not have been too serious except for the fact that I had just one nickel—just *one* nickel—in my pocket. I had been counting on the return ticket that was usually provided. There was nothing to do now but walk the few miles, about twelve I believe, to Evanston where the Chicago Elevated system reached its northern terminus. However the fare on that conveyance was *ten* cents. I had never panhandled in my life, but perhaps this was the time to start. I thought deeply about this on that long, dreary, and most uncomfortable trip on freezing feet. The more I thought the less attractive became the idea of asking a stranger for even just a nickel. Then I suddenly remembered that I had an acquaintance in Evanston—a youngish lady I had met on my voyage to France. Through correspondence we had kept in touch, and on my return to the States we had met a few times in Chicago. I had not seen her lately, but I felt sure she would welcome a call from me. I could tell her a plausible story about losing my wallet, and this would solve my dilemma. I would not have to humiliate my ego; after all an innocent little lie would be better than asking a stranger for help.

In Evanston I found a phone booth, deposited my nickel, and dialed the number. The phone at the other end rang: it rang, and rang, and rang, interminably it seemed. Obviously, there was no one home. Exasperated by this added turn of bad luck, I slammed down the receiver with considerable force. There was an instantaneous rain of coins in the return box. I was stupefied with wonder by this sudden change of heart from the gods, whoever they might be. I collected all of eighty-five cents in coins—a veritable bonanza in my situation. I immediately sought warmth, hot food, and drink before boarding the "El" for home. (This was in 1930, when the dollar was worth at least five times what it is today.)

Another Hitch

Mrs. Teich was most solicitous and apologetic about what had happened to cause my fruitless trip, but of course she never knew the extent of the consequences. However, there were some other, more serious circumstances that interfered with and delayed my finishing work on the portrait. First, Mrs. Teich fell ill with a flu virus and was unable to pose for several weeks. Unfortunately, time was not the only thing lost. Mrs. Teich shed more than a few pounds during her illness, and this wrought a substantial change in her appearance from that shown in the painting, which had been nearing completion. When we discussed this, she confessed that she was greatly pleased by her loss of poundage. She said she was determined to never regain what she had lost, and she fervently hoped I could alter the portrait to correspond to her improved image. This, of course, was not an easy task. It required several more sittings and a great deal of sweat on my part. However, before I could call the picture finished to my satisfaction, there came another hitch.

The Teichs had planned a vacation trip in Europe. They left in early June and were away for five weeks. When they returned, to my dismay, and I suppose to hers, Mrs. Teich, in spite of her resistance, had regained her previous girth. I had to build her up again to her original dimensions. What an inspiration-killing seesaw this had become! If I should ever develop any inclination to become a professional portrait painter, which seems doubtful at best, recollection of this episode would surely dispel it.

But the day finally arrived when "ze job" was finished and presented for approval. I was happy that the reaction of the whole family was very favorable, but I couldn't resist wondering if they might not be just as relieved as I was that the long, drawn-out project was ended at last. The portrait was ultimately surrounded with an elaborately carved gold frame, which I could not consider very appropriate; but it was obviously very expensive, and I consoled myself that it served to demonstrate what the patron thought of the painting's worth.

A Small Fortune

When I was asked to present a bill for my efforts I was at sea. On one hand there were the seemingly endless delays that had prolonged the work interminably, not to mention the discomforts I suffered; on the other were the numerous kindnesses and courtesies to consider: the train tickets and the intermittent hospitality of bed and board over that long period. A businesslike calculation was impossible from my standpoint. I let Mr. Teich know that I would have to leave this detail entirely in his hands, and that I would be satisfied with any sum he might consider fair. He mailed his check for $500—a very handsome and generous settlement I thought. To me, this represented a small fortune, and it actually was, considering the value of the dollar during that period. Although I was sure the Teichs were well satisfied with the portrait, I was not too happy with it. I considered it a good likeness and interpretation of character, but I felt that in its having been reworked drastically twice, it had lost the freshness and spontaneity that my enthusiasm had begun to express initially. Still, the experience had been both enjoyable and enlightening. It also had allowed me to exist as an artist, whereas without it I might well have failed to pursue what I considered my destiny.

But $500, bounteous as it seemed, lasted a discouragingly short time. I had forgotten about some bills I owed and the dilapidated state of my very limited wardrobe. Most of the latter was threadbare and definitely required replacement. In addition, my supply of colors, canvas, and other necessary materials had to be replenished if I was to produce the works I had in my head. It was autumn and I began to be depressed again about prospects for my survival as an artist during the coming winter. At this moment and many others like it I was assailed with doubt about the future—not just my own, but that of my friends in the arts as well. Such moments would always lead to a bitter philosophical discontent with the status of the arts, as affected by the economy and the political situation. There was nothing unusual in this. Other artists, and in fact the whole of society, were beginning to sorely doubt what the future might have in store for America as a whole. The term *depression* applied not only to the economy—it applied as well to the mental state of the nation as a whole.

A Hard Life in the Harlan Mines

"Sudy" Gates

Historically, one of the most exploited workers has been the miner. This was especially true during the Great Depression when finding any other job was difficult. The working conditions for miners above and below ground were terrible. The hours were long and the pay was dismal. The industry owned everything around the mines including the miners' homes. The miners' families were even forced to patron the company store which sold overpriced living necessities that could be bought on credit. After paying high prices for housing and other living expenses every month, the miner could actually find himself owing his employers money. Children were sometimes brought into the mines to work alongside their parents to try and make up the difference.

The coal fields in Harlan, Kentucky, had some of the worst working conditions in the country. After the National Miners Union moved in to organize the workers, many bloody conflicts followed that resulted in a number of deaths. But the conflicts focused much unwanted attention on the mine owners and resulted in public investigations and changes in the treatment of employees. The following transcript is from Mistress "Sudy" Gates, the wife of a miner, who is speaking before the National Committee for the Defense of Political Prisoners. The National Committee was a labor organization dedicated to supporting the worker's right to organize and protest in any legal means allowed. Renowned American author John Dos Passos records the session.

Excerpted from "Sudy" Gates's account in *Harlan Miners Speak: Report on Terrorism in the Kentucky Coal Fields,* by Members of the National Committee for the Defense of Political Prisoners. Copyright © 1932 by Harcourt Brace and Co. Reprinted with permission from Harcourt, Inc.

In the name of the Women's branch of the National Miners Union of Straight Creek, we welcome the writers' committee. We are glad to know that some one outside of Straight Creek is interested in the conditions of the miners in Straight Creek and we thank them very much for this interest.

It is hard to explain to them just exactly the conditions of the lives of the miners here. Our wages are so small that we cannot buy anything, just barely what we have to have and just what we can exist on. We . . . the miners' wives have to go to the stores to draw the scrip what their husbands made the day before; probably they could get some and probably not. If they got any they only got a small allowance.

The biggest part is taken out for carbide [the fuel used in the miners' lighting].

They cannot get much to eat because they have to buy this.

We are glad to have this writers' committee to investigate these things and probably it will be known and help us in time to come.

Poor Conditions

When we go to the company stores the prices are so high, we cannot buy our groceries or anything. Our children, they go without lunch. Sometimes they have a little beans and corn bread but without anything on it.

We have all kinds of disease because of that. No nourishment or food. That is the reason why we have Flux. There are many cases of Flux. We don't even know how many. We have had many deaths because of the conditions of food.

The conditions of our drinking water is so impure that the county nurse reported that it was very bad and impure, yet we have not better water yet. The nurse, when she took a test of the water, the doctor asked her what she was doing taking the test of the water. The doctor asked her what she was doing taking the test, why she was taking this test and that it was his business to take this test. She said it was not his business but hers and she was going to do it.

The conditions of our houses are very bad. We have to pay $3.00, $5 to $6.40 a month rent for them. The houses are so bad they are about to fall down. So rotten and cold, we nearly freeze to death. You can ask the boss to fix the house but he tells us he cannot and won't do it.

Also I have something else about the doctor. There was a case of a little kid. The doctor saw it and said nothing was wrong, to give it a dose of castor oil. It was sick for many weeks and one day they asked the doctor what was the matter with the baby and he said there was no chance for the baby to live, and then when he saw the funeral of the kid he said, "Did that kid finally die and git out of the way?"

That is the kind of a doctor we have here.

We are cut wages for the doctor; the men are cut two dollars a month for the doctor. You get very bad service from the doctor.

What's the good of calling a doctor, if he doesn't come around when you call him? You call him one day and he doesn't come around for a few days. You can be dead in the meantime.

And the company, if they know a man is honest and pays back his debts, then they give him a scrip and get him into debt and then he works and works and pays the debt. And then if he refuses to get in debt then they won't let him work.

We go to Pineville to buy where the stuff is much cheaper but he doesn't want us to go there, but he wants us to buy in his store and if we refuse, he doesn't let us work for him; so we have to do it. When we git scrip we have to buy in his store and we have to pay much more for everything and then we can't buy anything after we pay for the carbide.

The National Miners Union, which has come into this country, we never realized what it was to have some one help us until they came in here and got us poor miners together.

Stick Together

There are so many miners here that we don't know what wages is. They have gotten up to four dollars or five dollars a day, but now they get two dollars to three dollars and the miners must organize and must organize their wives. The wives must be organized because she has to suffer, she and the children has to go without clothes and she has to see her children starve. It is time for the miners to organize and to stick together to fight these conditions.

The miners yet cannot see when they won't need their bosses.

The thing for every one is to unite and stick together and fight these conditions and fight for better wages and better food and more of it and milk and stuff for the children.

The children are so cold, they turn blue. They try to go to school and try to learn but they have not got the energy to learn.

We have to fight these wage cuts. Every time you turn around you get a wage cut. Every time they cut the prices in the store a little, we know that we are going to get a wage cut. They cut the prices a little bit and give us a big wage cut.

That is the reason we must organize a union and stick together to fight this thing.

The wives here, you don't see a one that has sufficient clothes to go out in public. Their shoes is off their feet. They have them tied with strings. In the summer, if they happen to have a pair of shoes, they don't wear them, they save them for the cold winter. The kids they go around with no shoes and no food, do you wonder why we are losing children?

I don't see how they can stand it. It is hard for grown persons to stand.

Many people say, Why don't you buy? We have nothing to buy with. If we git some money, we go to the store and when we buy, we can't buy less than 25 cents worth of carbide and we have to buy the carbide.

I ask all the women and all the men of this place to stick together. All the wives must join with us. Now is the time that the women has some right to fight with her husband and by both fighting we can win in time to come.

The good thing about the National Miners Union is that they don't leave the women out and so, not like in the other times, many times the wives would make the husbands go back to work. The wives must meet with their husbands and together plan, because it is as much to the wives as to the miners. In the National Miners Union the wives know just as much what is going on. We are not going to say, "Go on, Johnny, go back to work"

We are going to stand right along with them and fight.

We are thankful to the National Miners Union for this. It makes you have a sensation you hardly know what it is all about. We never had nothing to do before but cook some beans. Now we have something to do. Now we have something else to do. We are going to have John win the strike. We were naked long enough and we are going to fight for something. We are going to keep this organization and we are going to fight.

Chapter 4

Out on the Farms

Chapter Preface

Even before the Depression, U.S. farmers had been in trouble. Low prices and drought contributed to a national crisis. Farmers lost everything, and foreclosures became frighteningly common. In response, groups of militant farmers in the Midwest attended foreclosure auctions with the intention of bullying prospective buyers so that they would not bid on family fortunes. The intimidation could lead to a lynching if the buyers were not easily cowed. Once the prospective buyers had given up, the farmers would repurchase the farm and any equipment for pennies on the dollar, then give them back to the original owners.

The U.S. Communist Party and other labor groups jumped at the opportunity presented in the Midwest. If a revolution could be started anywhere, it would be in one of the most hard-struck areas of the country. Labor organizers helped rally farmers for protests and offered leadership. But to most farmers, the political agenda of the Communist Party was unimportant. They just wanted to be able to make a decent living and provide for their families.

In the panhandle region of the United States, overcultivation had ruined the land. The dry topsoil was blown off the plains into the sky. Farmers from Oklahoma, Texas, Kansas, Colorado, and New Mexico abandoned their farms, and many of them traveled to California. Upon arriving, they experienced many hardships and found the farming culture completely different than what they had left behind. But they had no place else to go, so they endured the discrimination from locals and the low pay. Eventually, the hastily built shantytown communities nicknamed "Okievilles" were integrated into the California towns they surrounded.

In the South, tenant farmers and sharecroppers made up 50 percent of all farmers. They had always been an exploited class. Tenancy was an outdated institution from the southern plantation system that allowed landless farmers to lease a portion of land in exchange for a share of the crops. Many of the landowners took advantage of their tenants, who often could not read. They skewed agreements in their favor, which made it difficult for tenants to survive, and sold them supplies and daily necessities at marked-up costs. Many tenants moved regularly in hopes of finding a better deal. Roosevelt's Agricultural Adjustment Act (AAA), which sought to raise prices by reducing production, actually made life even harder for tenants. Many landowners used the federal subsidy to buy tractors, and then released the tenant from their agreements. The tractor allowed landowners to work faster and cheaper than they could with tenants. Roosevelt later created the Bankhead-Jones Farm Tenancy Act in 1937 and the succeeding Farm Security Administration, but neither could really help the marginal farmer, who continued to be taken advantage of by landowners.

The Small Farmer Has Got It Much Harder

Jackson Bullitt

In the rural South over half of all farmers were tenant farmers.
Tenant farmers didn't own any land. They rented a portion of
land to farm in exchange for a share of their harvest. Many
landowners exploited their tenants and took advantage of
them. In the following WPA interview, Jackson Bullitt, a small
landowner in North Carolina, discusses the tenant system and
the government's attempts to control prices with subsidies.

I was born over near Juniper, Virginia, where I worked on
my father's farm till I was free. Then I moved to Deer
Run in North Carolina and rented a small farm for three
years. From there I moved to the old Anson place four miles
from Hilton, buyin' the house and little farm the next year.
I soon met Miss Della Huges, who lived in the neighborhood, and after a year we were married. What success I've
had I feel like I owe most of it to her; she was close and
savin' and helped me accumulate enough to pay for our
place and buy a little land every now and then. From own-
in' nothin', from bein' just a renter, I now own two farms, a
comfortable dwelling and three tenant houses, and some
town property in Hilton.

Since my wife died eleven years ago, though, I've not
done much, not even hardly held my own. My five girls has

done the best they could for me, but a man needs a companion to get along any sort o' how. I've been with two or three girls since Della left me, and I'd have married the widow woman if my daughters hadn't objected so strong. At one time she'd've had me too, but Mary was so rank against it I kept puttin' it off. Now I'm in no fittin' fix to get married— and Mary's married and gone, as well as Lela. I still love to talk to the widow, to be in her company. They say Mr. Forsythe is about to cut me out, but I don't think she'll have him; she would've had me, at one time. I met a girl I liked when I was visitin' Mary at Ocean View last summer, but of course it couldn't amount to nothin'. I don't know whether I'd've had this stroke or not if I had gone on and got married like I wanted to. Worry over losin' my wife and bein' alone, as well as other things, brought on the high blood pressure and the stroke that crippled me up like I am now. It's a helpless feelin' after you've been workin' and goin' hard all your life to be in this fix. Yesterday I drug this leg out to the wood pile and throwed some wood in the house out of the weather; today I ain't hardly able to move around.

About thirteen years ago we moved from the old place up here closer to Hilton so the children would be more convenient to the school and church. I was makin' right good money farmin' along then; in just one year I built and paid for this house we live in. One time I could've bought the place for $600, but when I did buy it cost me $3,200. Mary, Lela, and Selma went to Chowan College [Baptist women's school, Murfreesboro, North Carolina], and the two oldest ones taught a while before they got married. My youngest one, Lavinia, will soon get through her nurse's course in Norfolk. Lily does the best she can keepin' house for me, but she's afflicted and can't do like the others. If Selma's husband just hadn't got drowned last summer—but I'm thankful Selma and Lavinia were rescued, for they had a close call down there at the beach. Selma's husband aimed, after he finished his crop down at Buckner, to come here and take hold of the farm for me, which. would've been a fine arrangement all around. If Selma didn't have that cafeteria job at Hilton school now, I reckon she'd go crazy, losin' her husband just six weeks after marryin' him.

A Good Relationship with the Tenants

In spite of bein' paralyzed, I manage my farmin' pretty good, because I've got tenants I can trust. Sharecroppin' is the best system for this country I think; anyhow it's best for me. I don't know what I'd do if we had to go back to hirin' day labor altogether. Bob Miller, a white man, has been with me nineteen years. I've got confidence in him. He works a two-horse crop and always pays out and makes a little money besides. In fact, he has made enough clear some years to buy him a house and farm easy, but instead he lets his money get away from him somehow, with nothin' much to show for it. It used to worry me for Bob to throw away his money, but my wife would say: "Why should you care? If he saved up his money, he wouldn't work for you, and you'd lose a good tenant." That is one way to look at it.

From March to December I furnish Bob $4.00 a week for himself, his wife, and the child they took to raise; they've got no children of their own. My time price is 10 percent, which is understood between me and Bob; that's fair, and all tenants are willin' to pay 10 percent for the use of the money. Bob furnishes his team, while I pay for the fertilizer. I let him run the farm to suit himself, goin' down there to see about him only once or twice a month. This year, which was the hardest we've had in some time, Bob paid out all right and cleared $200.

My men always clear a little somethin', though I don't see how Miles Richards did this year. With nobody but him to plow and with him pushin' seventy and not well either, it's right hard on Miles. He's been with me two years and is stayin' on again. Looks like when I get a man I generally keep him, if he's any 'count at all. I rather have white sharecroppers every time. For one thing you can trust 'em with your team and with havin' more judgment about runnin' a farm than colored tenants do. It seems to come natural for the colored ones to be a little roguish, while you can put

confidence in the white farmer that way. Most of the stealin'
you hear landlords complain about, though, is the landlord's
fault as much as the tenant's. When the landlord takes short-
cuts and deals unfair, the tenant knows it, even if he can't
put his finger on where the cheatin' is; that's where, as a
general rule, he takes to stealin'. I never had no stealin',
practically none, to contend with. Tenants I've had to get rid
of after a year were usually impudent or triflin', wouldn't
work the crop to no advantage. Colored tenants worry you
too sometimes about their old superstitious notions; some
wouldn't plant to bless you except on the moon. Some white
ones are that way, of course, but I've not had them to contend with so far.

*A tenant farmer sits outside his home in North Carolina. Because they rented
land to farm, tenant farmers only kept a portion of the goods they grew.*

Miles Richards made one bale of cotton on his farm this
year, and just half of it goes to him. His wife helps him what
she can, but she has been to the asylum and can't be counted on. One daughter is married, and the single one—she just
as well to be. She's come back home on Miles now, with her
baby, and that's another one for Miles to feed. She's a good-
lookin' girl, too; it's a pity she threw herself away. Miles

told me the other day that it takes $2.00 a week to buy milk for the baby. There's the little girl, too, that Miles and his wife took to raise. That's one thing about sharecroppers; they never seem to have too many children to feed and clothe but what they can find a place for one more. They're goin' to have children—and yes, dogs too—around 'em. Miles furnishes himself; how he does it I don't know, but that was his request. He's bound to owe somebody more than he can pay, the way his expenses are. I think it's better for the landlord to furnish so much money a week or month to run the tenant than it is to furnish ration like use to be done. The tenant can trade to much better advantage that way and feel more free too, I think.

My other man is John Winder, colored, who I hire by the day. He lives yonder across the field and works here around the house—cuttin' wood, feedin' the stock, tendin' to the outdoor jobs I use to enjoy doin', as well as workin' in the field on my own home farm. I give him sixty cents a day and a pea patch, a house to live in, and board from my table. I think that's fair.

I reckon I run my business a little different from most landlords. For one thing, I require the tenants to keep a set of books too. Every time I enter an item in my book I make them set it down in theirs as well. So when settlement time comes, they know good as I do how the expenses are goin' to run out. I never had no trouble settlin' in my life; sometimes maybe there'll be a difference of a dollar or two the tenant failed to enter like I told him, but he'll remember soon as it's called to his attention. All the tenants ought to be required to keep books just like the landlord and know exactly what's charged against them and what for. Then, too, I always let my sharecroppers have half the peanut vines, as well as pay my half to hire the peas picked off. They say I'm the only landlord in this country that pays my half of the pea-picker expense, but it's the only fair way, looks like to me. When it comes to ditchin' or other labor for permanent improvement on the farms, I always pay for that; some of the landlords kick because the tenant won't ditch his own farm, but I reckon that's our business. For repair work around the house, I furnish the timber and the nails and let the tenant do the work he's usually willin' if he's any 'count at all, to do that.

Peanuts Saved Me This Year

If it hadn't been for peanuts this year, I'd have gone in the hole sure enough. On 75 acres of open land, not countin' the acres I rented to the government, I made 5 bales of cotton and 400 bags of peas. Before the boll weevil hit here so bad, I used to make 16, 17, and 18 bales of cotton and 600 bags of peas. So many things has knocked the farmer late years. Like the rest, I got excited and bought one of them dustin' machines the year the boll weevil first got rank here. That had to be junked, for we found the dustin' wa'n't worth a cent. Then the value of land has been cut to half, though the taxes ain't been lowered to take care of the decreased valuation. The same thing is true of my town property, the store buildin' I rent for $20 a month. I invested $6,000 in it and now couldn't sell it for half that. The rent don't near pay the interest, the taxes, and repairs on this investment. On the side I used to make a little money sellin' peanuts, but a fellow in Hilton undermined me when a new boss took the place of the one I had been dealin' with for years, promisin' more business to the peanut concern than I had been handlin'. I still sell peanut bags, though there's not much in it now since I'm handicapped about gettin' around. I have to depend on Selma to drive for me.

Not Much Help

The government farm program hasn't helped me much. Roosevelt's intentions are good; I've no doubt of that, and I'd vote for him again if *he* was all that was involved. But the way things are in this country, you've got to have a pull with the ring crowd to get anything out of the government rentals. Some big farmers has profited by it. One county commissioner, that kept the farm agent in when he was on his way out for too much political activity, has been able to buy a farm a year because of his pull with the farm agent's office since then. Others has made a big thing out of it too. They manage to get 500 pounds to the acre, while the little fellows has to take much less. I got only 300 pounds to the acre last year, and some that don't have a bit bigger yield than I do get 500 pounds without any trouble.

Then there's the question of rentin' land to the government. Some say the farmers can't cheat because of the map they've got over in Leesburg. Well, they do just the same. Some cut down bushes in uncleared land, sowed it in velvet beans that run up rank and tall and covered up the stumps, and then rented this land to the government. That happened just down the road on a certain fellow's farm. One man that has just cut the pulpwood off a piece of land aims to sow it down in beans this year and draw government rent. All I drawed last year for co-opin' with the government was $25, and half of that went to the sharecroppers.

It's right, I think, for the sharecroppers to get half the two government checks. Some don't think they ought to share in the spring check, though they wouldn't kick on the parity check.[1]

I don't know; I don't get enough to lose no sleep over it either way. I believe in fair dealin's, and it's enough to make folks sore to see how some gobble it up, how farmers linked up with the political ring in Jackson [the county seat, Northampton County] are gettin' rich on the government. I don't want a cent don't belong to me from the government or nobody else. I want the tenant to have his share fair and honest, and I don't think you'll find one that'll say I cheated him. The Golden Rule is the method I've tried to farm by with my sharecroppers. The only problem I see is for folks

---

1. To improve farm prices in the 1930s, the federal government paid farmers (with the "spring check") to reduce the amount of land they farmed and (with parity checks) the amount of crops they produced. Tenant farmers believed that they should receive both payments since, although they were not landowners, their acreage and their output had been reduced. Landowners usually favored sharing only the parity checks with their tenants, and this was the general practice. Some landowners defrauded their tenants by keeping both checks. Thus, even when fraud was not involved, a New Deal program favored the more prosperous and more powerful.

to do right. There'll be a few worries along, for tenants can be aggravatin', but a man's children even can aggravate him, so that's just a part of it. When it comes to gettin' 'em out of jail, standin' their bond, buyin' their coffins—well, I'm always thankful it ain't my children I'm havin' to do it for. By happen-chance, I've not had that kind of thing to do for my tenants much. I'm good to them, and they're good to me.

Speakin' of the farm program, I'll have to say the government has helped the peanut farmers by takin' the peas off their hands, storin' them in bonded warehouses, and allowin' them three and a quarter cents for them. Otherwise, peas would have been dirt cheap and many a farmer would have lost his place for debt. Peanuts is all that has paid expenses the past two years. The farmers are wantin' now to plant more peas, which will run the price down like cotton, though they seem to think the government will protect them. If I had a barn I'd plant some tobacco too, but barns are too expensive to build under the present uncertainty. Lots of farmers around here aim to plant some tobacco this year, since there's no tobacco control now. The boll weevil has discouraged the cotton farmers so they're bound to shift to some other crops some. But it's hard for us around Hilton to get away from cotton; we say we are goin' to cut, but when the time comes to plant we turn back to cotton or would if 'twa'n't for government control. The high cost of fertilizin' the cotton crop has disgusted farmers, as well as has the boll weevil; with the heavy fertilizin' farmers have practiced they can't hope to make much more than expenses under boll-weevil conditions. There used to be a time when farmers lived more at home than they do today. Why, now they even burn coal instead of wood.

The prospects for farmers look very gloomy to me at present. But we've pulled out of a lot of bad situations in the past, and maybe it'll be better than we think for. Eighteen eighty-nine was a bad year when farmers thought they was ruined, but cotton has been as high as forty cents a pound since that year. By 1950—but a lot of us won't have to worry about cotton by that time.

United in the Fields

Ella Reeve Bloor

By 1933, over 150,000 farms were being lost to foreclosure every year, a disproportionate amount of which were in Iowa. A movement called the Farmers Holiday Association began in Iowa with a peaceful strike by farmers who withheld their products from market. But the association became more militant, and it soon set up roadblocks to keep trucks from delivering any produce or dairy products to the market. They also banded together at foreclosure auctions and bullied buyers away from the sales so they could reclaim the farms and return them to the original owners. The auctions became known as "penny sales" since many of the properties went for pennies on the dollar.

Ella Reeve Bloor, also known as "Mother Bloor," was a well-known Communist Party leader who spent most of her life organizing labor. She was very active during the Depression, helping to lead the United Farmers' League. The UFL supported the farmers by offering relief supplies to destitute farmers as well as organizing protests. The following excerpt from her biography describes her experiences with the Farmers Holiday Association and other groups as they tried to raise prices and keep farms from being foreclosed.

A long with the miners and textile workers, the farmers were a depressed section of the population all through the boom years. In the decade between 1920 and 1930, there was a crisis of "over production" (with millions starving), farm prices falling below the cost of production, and the number of farms decreasing by 150,466. During the year ending March 1, 1930, 20.8 out of every 1000 farms were lost through forced sales, foreclosures or bankruptcy. Hoover refused effective farm aid. His makeshift Agricultural Marketing Act was administered by a Farm Board made up of bankers, and prices continued to drop. The [Communist] Party's practical proposals for farm relief started many of the farmers thinking along new lines.

The Party was first to advance the demand for a sharp cut in the unreasonable spread between the low prices paid to the farmer and the high prices paid by the consumer. Other important proposals by the Party were support for these demands: "No more foreclosures. No evictions. No deficiency judgments. The farm family holds the first mortgage!" The Party also advocated cash relief for those in distress through no fault of their own, and close cooperation between the farmers and organized labor.

This campaign in North Dakota is personally memorable to me because of my marriage to that pioneer North Dakota farmer and good Communist, Andrew Omholt. He was district organizer of North and South Dakota and Montana, and we campaigned together, visiting towns as far as 700 miles from the headquarters in Minot, North Dakota.

The U.F.L. Is Born

After the election campaign was over, we helped organize the farmers into the United Farmers' League, an organization which paved the way for the great Farm Holiday movement. The Hoover depression had hit with particular severity the farmer on the dry plains of the Dakotas and the Great Lakes region of cut-over timber lands ruined by the lumber barons. The United Farmers' League appeared in this region to fight for the homes, equipment and livestock of thousands of farmers who had exhausted their resources.

Once in Frederick, we were called on by a farmer named Lutio who was about to be evicted by the bank from the family home where he had brought up seven children. The U.F.L. got together about seventy cars and drove down there. We told the sheriff and the banker they couldn't evict the Lutio family. The banker gave ten days' grace; then the new tenant would move in. We told him the Lutios would make room for the new tenant, but would keep on living there too. They had no place to go and no money. A week later I was asked to come down again, to explain to some 60 or 70 new people who had joined the U.F.L., as a result of our visit, how they should function. We held a big meeting before the cooperative gasoline station. The banker's seventeen-year-old son rounded up hoodlums to break up the meeting. They cat-called and booed me. But we had mobilized a group of powerful young Finns [immigrant farmers from Finland], and I announced, " You can stay here all night, but we're going to have this meeting." Presently the hoodlums disappeared. A big Finnish woman whispered to me, "They've gone to get the fire engine and hose." But I wasn't worried. I had seen our husky Finns detach themselves from the crowd and follow them. When the hoodlums reappeared with the fire engine and hose, there was a tug of war; somehow the hose got slit, and it was hoodlums who got the wetting. We had our meeting, and the Lutios were not evicted.

Crisis of Biblical Proportion

In 1931, the first of four successive years of drought, there was a severe grasshopper plague in the Dakotas. The Red Cross workers sent out from eastern cities to administer relief had very little understanding of the farmers and their needs. If a farmer drove up to the relief station in a battered old Ford, the Red Cross worker would say, "You can't have any relief if you can afford to drive here in a car." "But I had to drive twenty miles to get here," would be the answer. "Why didn't you use a horse?" "My horses are dead in the fields."

One very helpful action at that time was the following: North Dakota farmers took truckloads of lignite coal, very plentiful all over North and South Dakota, to exchange for hay. But when farmers in Red River Valley sent word to the United Farmers' League that they had a lot of potatoes, and if the men dug them we could have them to distribute, the

Red Cross refused to let us ship the potatoes we dug where we knew they were needed. However, our strong organization finally prevailed and directed the farmers to meet the carloads of potatoes wherever they were sent.

During the 1932 Presidential campaign which resulted in Roosevelt's election and in which [William Z.] Foster and [American Labor organizer Earl C.] Ford were the Party candidates, the big militant milk strike then going on in Iowa came up for discussion at a meeting of the Central Committee of the Party in New York. With crops a little better, prices for farm products had reached a record low. Strikes, which the farmers called "holidays," by which they meant a moratorium for evictions and foreclosures, were sweeping the farm areas, with Iowa as the storm center. Feeling that something must be done by our Party in recognition of the importance of the milk strike, I suggested that [my son Hal] should be sent out with me to Iowa to encourage the farmers. Milo Reno, president of the Farmers' Holiday Association had called the governors of seven states together in Sioux City, Iowa, to discuss moratoriums for farm debts. We feared his purpose was to break the strike, so successfully carried on by the farmers, and in which they had the cooperation of the workers of nearby cities, since the farmers gave the milk to the children of the unemployed instead of throwing it out when they stopped trucks trying to make deliveries to the big trusts.

We wired Hal to come to Des Moines, and met him there. After holding a big meeting in Des Moines, Hal, Rob Hall, who had joined us, and I drafted a set of resolutions for the Sioux City conference, dealing with such problems as the low price of milk at the milk sheds, and the spread between that and the price paid by the consumer; and a call for a convention of real dirt farmers in Washington to carry their problems direct to their congressmen. The meeting of governors was to take place in Sioux City next day and we were determined to get the ear of those farmers coming to town to tell the governors what they wanted.

We got up early the next morning and drove all day to

Sioux City, some two hundred miles away. The papers featured statements by Milo Reno that the strike was over, which we knew was not true, because the pickets were as lively as ever on the roads, and no milk was passing through. The governors had arrived and had put up at the largest hotel. A few days before, a county sheriff, near Sioux City, deputized over a hundred men to stop the pickets by force. But instead of the deputies stopping the unarmed pickets, it was the pickets who, with bare hands, took charge of the deputies, disarmed them, removed their coats, and sent them back in their shirt sleeves to Sioux City.

U.F.L. Grand Marshall

About 10 o'clock in the morning Hal, Rob Hall, and I drove out to the park where 10,000 farmers were already assembled. Towards noon the number swelled to about 15,000. They were milling around, apparently with no plans or leadership. I went up to one keen-looking farmer and asked, "Where are your leaders? You are Holiday members, aren't you?" "Yes, we are Holiday members, but I don't know whether or not we have any leaders. If we have, they must be up with the governors in the hotel." His tone was sarcastic. "Well," I said, "I am national organizer of the United Farmers' League of North Dakota, and have brought greetings from North Dakota. They are willing to cooperate in this strike in every way." The farmer's eyes popped. "Woman, can you speak?"

"A little."

He just took me by the shoulders and lifted me up on a table and said, "Shoot!"

In about a minute the farmers were around me in a solid mass, and I talked as I had never talked before. I told them not to listen to the governors' instructions to stop their fight just as they were gaining the victory, but to seize this opportunity to tell the governors their needs. They wanted me to go on and on and finally asked me to lead their parade.

That parade was something to remember. A cowboy band led it, followed by farm boys on horseback, and after them the prize truck. In it stood forty men, straight and proud, representing picket line Number 20—which had never let a truck go by. Behind Number 20 came the marching farmers. I was hoisted up on top of the truck cab. Perched up there precariously as we rode through the streets of Sioux City, I kept waving to the crowds with one hand, and trying to hold on with the other. I had often felt ready to die for the miners, but this time I was sure I was about to die for the farmers! The parade had a thunderous reception. Workers lining the streets shouted. "Boys, we are with you. We'll help you, and you help us!" We halted before the governors' hotel, and the farmers called out, "Come on, governors, send out your soldiers, we are ready." We could see them peeping out from behind the curtains and knew they were good and scared of these farmers.

Before the meeting had disbanded at the park, I had said, "Why not hold a meeting right in the hotel, draft resolutions to the governors, and tell them in an organized fashion what you want and why you want to continue the strike?" So now they marched right into the hotel auditorium, elected a chairman, and passed all the resolutions unanimously. The meeting ended with a call to the convention in Washington, and election of a committee to present the resolutions to the governors. The governors at first contemptuously refused to see the committee and didn't give in until about 9 o'clock. Late that night the newsboys ran through the streets shouting, "Extra! Extra! The farmers have the governors on the spot!" The resolutions, printed in the papers, made a great stir. The next day the farmers went on with their strike. We went out to their picket lines in the middle of the day. The women brought cooked dinners to the men, setting tables right by the roadside. We were invited to eat with them. Every time a milk truck came along, the men stopped eating, made the truck driver turn around and go back, and then returned to their dinners. They asked me to stand on the table and talk.

That night we visited another picket line. Here they had cleared a big space at a cross-roads, erected a temporary platform draped with flags, and wanted me to talk. Having no leadership from their own organization they were hungry for encouragement. As a farmer's wife from North Dakota, they accepted me as one of their own.

The Penny Sales

This was followed in Iowa by the period of the "penny sales," when the militancy of the organized farmers kept them on the land until they got their moratorium. At sheriff's sales, the farmers gathered, bid ten cents for a cow, ten cents for a plow, ten cents for the house, etc., allowing no other bids. Having bought the farmer's property, they gave it back to him again.

In Lamar, Iowa, thirty miles from Sioux City, a well-liked farmer was behind in his interest payments to an insurance company. The company lawyer came with the judgment note enabling the insurance company to put in a bid for the farm and take it over in case the farmers did not bid. The news went around like lightning. Two truckloads of Unemployed Council members joined the thousands of farmers assembled at the court house. They told the sheriff that he would not be able to sell the man out. "I must," he said, "or I will lose my job." Then they went to the lawyer and asked, "Have you got a judgment note?" "Yes," he told them. "You are not going to use it to bid with," they said. "I must," he cried, "or I will lose my job." The farmers took him out of the court house and stood him under a tree, and asked, "Will you write a telegram to your company and tell them to withdraw the note?" He said, "No, I can't do it." One old farmer said, "Get the rope." They didn't intend to use the rope, but they had one handy, threw it over the limb of the tree and repeated: "Will you send the telegram?" "Give me a paper and pencil!" He wrote: "Withdraw the note. My neck is in danger."

The Silent Protest

Another method the farmers used successfully to prevent evictions was the "silent protest." In Sioux City, the farmers packed the court room every month on the day set for the public sale of foreclosed farms and small homes. As he read each item on his list, the county treasurer would pause for bids. But the farmers there to save their neighbors' farms would just stand silently with grim smiles on their faces, and no bids would be made. Once a man ventured to bid, and the farmers quietly closed in on him and heaved him out with their shoulders, hardly moving, just pushing him along until he went through the door. Groups of unemployed workers came too to stand there with the farmers in case they were needed. At the end of December, the county treasurer said in disgust, "I've done my duty, but there's not a bid in the lot of you. The sales will be postponed until spring." The farmers never failed to appear to make their silent protest. It was the most convincing demonstration I ever saw of the power of solid, persistent organization.

Even after the moratorium law on farm debts was passed in Iowa, the judges kept on selling farms illegally. The farmers gathered in protest, were met by troops and some terrible fights occurred. One judge at Lamar who ignored the moratorium bill was taught a lesson by the farmers who took him out of his office one day and made him walk a mile in his B.V.D.'s [underwear].

I never saw anything like the militancy of those farmers. They were wonderful. Only on one occasion a few of them threatened to get out of hand. The National Guardsmen sent to Lamar were just high school boys—some of them farmers' sons. The night after their entry into Lamar, we heard a tramping up the stairs, and a bunch of hot-headed farmers came into our office saying, "How many men can you give us? What arms have you got?"

"Wait a minute, boys," I said. "We haven't any guns, you know."

"We can't stand having those young boys come and interfere with our rights—we're going to do something about it."

We made them sit down and talk it over. We told them we were preparing leaflets calling on Milo Reno to organize a big meeting of the Holiday Association in Des Moines, and rallies before the court houses in various counties to protest to the Governor against violations of the law and sending in the National Guard. We got them to see this was a better way than to go out and start a fight.

Within a week soldiers had raided our office, taken away baskets full of our papers, thrown our people into jail, arrested and held incommunicado a harmless old man who was distributing our leaflets. Andy and I were away at the time. They had planned to arrest us for inciting to riot when, as a matter of fact, it was we who had stopped a riot!

A National Conference

By the end of 1932 our work among the farmers had broadened out to such an extent that we were able to hold a highly successful Farmers' Emergency Relief Conference in Washington in December, 1932.

My son Hal was asked to help call such a conference by the Farm Holiday Committee in Sioux City. Some Nebraska Holiday members carried the news of the proposed conference back to their offices and it was enthusiastically supported. The call was quickly endorsed by Pennsylvania, New England and Alabama farm organizations, and became a real national conference. Working with Hal on the conference preparations were Lem Harris, Rob Hall, Otto Anstrom, and other active, intelligent young men who were familiar with the problems of the farmers.

Two hundred and forty-eight delegates from twenty-six states, representing thirty-three organizations and unorganized farmers attended the conference. It took place at the same time as the big march of the unemployed to Washington. The unemployed were being held outside the city by Hoover's police, and some were getting pneumonia and dying of exposure. The farmers' protests to their Congressmen were an important factor in finally getting the unemployed marchers into the city. The farmers themselves were treated courteously by their Congressmen, and even given a police escort into the city. . . .

One of the high points of that convention was the arrival of the sharecroppers' delegation from the South. They arrived a day late. Many of the farmers were living in tourist cabins down on the Potomac, only some of which were heated. The white farmers rushed to offer their heated cabins to the Negro delegates from the South, who they thought would suffer from the cold. The sharecroppers got a tremendous ovation at the convention. An Alabama sharecropper reported on the desperate conditions in his state, telling about the extreme poverty and the struggle for even the most elementary rights. A tactless delegate asked, "Tell us about the terror in the South," whereupon the speaker, who had lived for months under its shadow and was now near exhaustion from a sleepless and foodless journey, collapsed. We had to protect these sharecropper delegates from any publicity whatsoever, as their very lives were endangered by their attendance.

The conference raised demands for a moratorium on farm debts, and mapped out a program for militant action to improve farm conditions, including a struggle to prevent foreclosures, evictions and loss of farm property.

The convention voted to organize the Farmers' National Committee for Action, and to publish a weekly paper. The F.N.C.A. was a broad, united front movement taking in all kinds of farm organizations. I was asked to superintend the organization of the committee in five states—Montana, North and South Dakota, Iowa and Nebraska. Moving my headquarters to Sioux City, Iowa, I took up my work as secretary of the Farmers' Committee in these five states, Andy becoming organizer for the Sioux City district.

Following the Washington conference similar conferences and mass demonstrations took place in Nebraska, South Dakota, Iowa, and elsewhere. . . .

Further Progress

In November 1933, we held the second big F.N.C.A. conference in Chicago, heard reports of the success of the penny sales from many sections, and organized national legal defense work for farmers. The conference went even further than the Washington Conference by raising the demand for cancellation of secured farm debts of small and middle farmers, along with the stand against forced sales and auctions of impoverished families. It called for cash relief for destitute farm families, lowered taxes, measures to increase farmers' purchasing power, and abolition of oppression of Negroes. Here, with agricultural worker delegates present, we first brought vigorously to the fore the problems of agricultural workers. Our idea was to break down the antagonism between small farm owners and the agricultural workers. We made a special point of bringing the workers and farmers together at this convention, as in all our work. To drive home the point of workers' and farmers' unity, we wound up the convention by hiring a large auditorium for our final session, where thousands of Chicago workers cheered the farm delegates. The central section was reserved for the 702 farmer delegates from thirty-six different states. That meeting was a real demonstration of solidarity.

Next year, 1933–34, I was in Nebraska, bringing a message of encouragement and hope to these farmers triply stricken by drought, the dust storms that went with it, and low prices for farm products. It always seemed to me the farm women were the greatest sufferers. The choking, dust-filled air burns throat and eyes. It seeps inexorably into the houses, which have often been thrown out of plumb by high winds, leaving gaping chinks. Food, bed-clothing, furniture are all covered with a thick deposit, making it impossible to keep homes clean and tidy in the manner that these brave farm women would wish. Even their small and indispensable vegetable gardens are lost. Many a farm woman has carefully watered her small vegetable garden every evening in the hope of raising a few fresh vegetables only to have a hot dry wind blow a sand-blast which slithers the leaves and stops the growth of the plants. The combination of calamities to which these families were subjected would seem overwhelming, and yet they were in no sense beaten. We organized large groups of Nebraska farmers and found them just as militant as the farmers of Iowa.

Moving to the City

Calvin and Lola Simmons

> The farms of the Midwest and the South were having prob-
> lems well before the stock market crash. Years of drought and
> overcultivation had made the earth virtually useless. The
> farmers could not even grow enough to feed themselves. The
> onset of the Depression just made things worse. Many farm-
> ers and their families abandoned their worthless land and
> moved into the cities and towns looking for jobs. Conditions
> were seldom better in urban areas so most of them ended up
> on relief. Calvin and Lola Simmons were refugees from the
> mountains of Tennessee. They worked for years sharecrop-
> ping but were never able to get ahead. They moved to
> Knoxville and eked out a marginal living doing odd jobs.
> Their story was recorded by Dean Newman, Jennette
> Edwards, and James Aswell for the WPA record.

Calvin and me come from the mountains, for Calvin
knowed he could make a living in some way or another about town doing odd jobs. So we left the farm. We fared
on down to Knoxville. Our times has not been easy here.
But then times has always been hard with us. We was both
born poor. Lived poor all our lives. All in all, though, it's a
lots easier making out here than it was back there on the
farm. We ain't never had to ask a penny off of no one. Never asked the government to put us on relief, neither. . . .

Calvin's handy with tools . . . and always has been. He can
fix a chair or whatever kind of furniture you've got that looks
past doing, and it will be stout as new. He can build things,

just anything, from the ground up. He's good on porches and stairs steps. Most anything about a house that needs righting, Calvin can git it in shape. He does a heap of patching screens and painting roofs. He's not a regular plumber and electrician but he does some of that work, too. . . .

A New Home

This place here we live in, it's not any great shakes of a place. But we're going to stay on as long as we can. Every time we've moved from here to somewheres on the edge of town, Calvin's lost work. Here he's in close-catch of town folks that wants a job done right off. The biggest trouble about living in a basement like this is they's not any room for spreading. Well, three rooms is enough for me and Calvin and Cap, even if they're not big rooms. This here sitting room is space enough to hold the parlor furniture and Cap's bed. Cap's just only fifteen but he's near outgrowed that bed back yonder. He has to lay catercorners of it now. Ought to be some way Calvin could stretch it out, seems to me. I don't see no way we could put a double bed in that space even if we had cash to buy it—which we ain't.

Me and Calvin takes the back room. They's no grate in it, but some heat comes from the kitchen. That kitchen has a sink with running water, and that's the closest we ever come to having a bathroom. Well-a-day, not having such means less to us than most. Coming from the mountains, we is use to a wash pan and a tub for cleaning up. We has a halfway sort of a little water privy in the kitchen closet, but it don't flush right. I can tell you, though, it beats trotting out in the back yard in the weather.

The last of the three rooms we has is damp and cold without you keep a fire going all the time. And we can't do that. The basement's about all that's brick about the whole house. That's the reason our rooms stays that way. The house up above us is in awful shape. The roof leaks. It lets the water come right down the side of the walls. When a hard rain comes they's water all over the kitchen floor. I just reach the broom out. I keep sweeping it to the back door. The walls stay so wet half the time that wallpaper just pops off everywhere. . . .

I guess we can't expect just a whole lot for the rent we pay. The landlord never misses coming a Monday for our two-fifty. But fixing things up is another tale and it's never told. He won't do a blessed thing about this wetness and it matters not how much we howl. Tells us now that the government is planning to tear down every house in the block and put up some sort that ain't tenements. Well, 'twon't be no trouble to tear down. Just give a push, and not such a hard one neither, and the last one of these houses will come down and never a wrecking tool needed to help out. And the neighborhood is worse and far worse than the houses. Oh, I know it's no place to bring a youngin up at all. I thank the Lord that me and Calvin has got but only the one, and that's Cap. We can manage him all right with both of us studying on it. Most of the families in this block has from six all the way to ten youngins, and all sizes. Seems like about half of the mothers is sick. They just let the youngins run around as filthy as cow-dab. I tell you, most of these youngins learn to cuss and swear and take the Lord's name in vain when they's buggers of five years old and less. They start fighting amongst one another. Before long the mas and pas take sides. It ends in a cutting scrape or one or the other taking their leave of the street. Me and Calvin stays clear of it all.

We don't want no more trouble with neighbors. That's the main reason we moved from the mountains. Trouble with neighbors. Trouble betwixt Calvin and the Osmans over what they'd done to Calvin's coon dog. Drum was a night-running dog and I will freely admit it, but he wasn't a chicken-killer. Calvin had trained him about chickens to where he'd leave them alone. Why, I've seen that Drum flatten out on his belly and whine like he was scared to death if a chicken so much as passed him near. Calvin had trained him so he was really feared of a chicken. But it was something using around the Osman's place of nights and taking their hens. So they says 'twas Calvin's Drum. They'd shot him but they dassn't, for they just knowed what a hasty-passioned man my Calvin can be when it comes to his coon dog. So they tried one of their sneaky tricks. They caught Drum off in the woods and they docked his tail right slam up against his rump and they cropped his ears down to his head.

Calvin flat-out accused them Osmans of doing the job. They swore they didn't, but you could see the daylight through what they said. So it was a hardness sprung up and before long Calvin hopped all over an Osman and beat the corn out of him. Then the whole tribe ganged on him and came close to beating him to death. Looked like it was going to have to be a killing on one side or other. We didn't have enough kin to fight that Osman bunch. Calvin and me both knowed wasn't room for him and the Osmans on the same mountain. So me and him pulled out and come faring down from the mountains to Knoxville, and ain't never going back again. . . .

I miss them mountains sometimes. Yes, I miss that steep old land.

Me and Calvin growed up in the same neighborhood. The schools wasn't much we went to. Still they learned us to read and they learned us to write and how to say words as we should in talking. Calvin and me took a heartburning for each other when we was in that school. Then Mammy died and I come down to Knoxville and I got me a job in a steam laundry here. No place there or home for me, for Pappy brought in a new wife and started in on a new bunch of youngins. I made four dollars a week. Worked ten hours a day in the damp wash end. It wouldn't be a dry rag on me at the end of them ten hours. Most of us that worked there was girls come in from the country and down from the mountains. We managed by rooming together and doing all our own cooking and washing. Now, you hear folks talk a heap about the way country girls goes on with men when they come to the city. Ah, Lord! We was so wore out by time work hours was over that we was good and glad to fall into bed and sleep. At the laundry I worked up to the finishing room and I made five dollars and fifty cents. But the hours was longer and I was so tired all the time I'd just as soon been dead and done with it.

Well and all, it was right after the war that Calvin come down from the mountains. He talked me into going back and keeping house for him. It didn't take a powerful lot of talk. I was sick and tired of working like a slave. But I guess I'd sort of lost track of things I'd once knowed about living on a farm. That's a hard life. Anyhow, I went. I never had it in my mind that it was a thing wrong about me going. But the neighbors talked about us living together. Five years after I went to keeping house for Calvin, Cap come. I don't see no difference in the way me and Calvin feels about Cap because we never did have the time nor money to git a preacher or justice of peace to say a few words over us. It costs a lot of money to git married. More than five dollars some places. We never seen five dollars ahead till we come down here to Knoxville. Then it seemed like a plumb fool waste of money. They tell me that some good lawyer says a common-law marriage is just as good as a church or court one any day. So I ain't noways ashamed that me and Calvin has never got around to the regular kind. He's past fifty and I'm near to it and ain't neither of us ever trotted around loose like half the ones that blows about wedlock and such. We is poor but we's decent.

Farm Work Versus City Work

Being poor ain't easy nowheres, but it's a sight better in the city than on a farm. City folks just don't know nothing at all about what country folks puts up with. Me and Calvin rented the farm we had in the mountains. It looked like it took the biggest part of what come from it to just meet the rent. Every cent from the tobacco crop went for rent.

We never did git ahead to the point of having stock of our own. Had to borrow from the neighbors. That meant they'd git theirs plowed when the weather was right. Even if the ground was as hard as a brick, Calvin had to do plowing when he could borrow some mules or some horses. I didn't git nowhere trying to make extry with a garden. Pigs and chickens seemed like two things it just wasn't no way for us to keep from dying. The sort of cows we could pay for wasn't worth the feeding. We's had more butter and milk and meat and eggs here in town than we ever see on that farm. Farm living is plain slaving from one month to the next, from morning to night. And they's nothing left to show for all the hard work you do. Winter comes and you got to start toting wood for the fires. Have to tote it yourself when they's no sign of horse or mule to help you. Then every bit of the water you've a use for must be drawed from a well or fotch [fetched] to the house from a spring. Here all you have to do is twist at the hydrant and out pours the water. Neither one of us ever wants to go back to farming.

Calvin gits plenty of work here in Knoxville. He works cheap and that's the reason, I guess. He's not what you'd call a skilled worker. But he can do as good work as the best of them, I don't care what name you call them by.

They's more folks here in Knoxville that wants cheap repairing than any other kind. The rich folks is the same way. Calvin knows where he can git supplies cheap. He can take a contract lower than most and still come out on top. If he could just go straight from one job to the next, why, I bet he'd make close to twenty dollars a week. Like things is now, he makes about ten. He loses money looking for jobs and figgering on gitting things in shape to git the contract. Old customers has always stuck with him. But things ain't going to keep dropping to pieces about the same folks' house if they's fixed right. And Calvin always fixes them right. Sort of cuts his own throat, but he does it.

I do all the washing and ironing and cleaning and cooking. And I can stretch that ten dollars out for the three of us. Rent and coal and kindling and food eats up about seven of it. That leaves three for other things and the clothes we wear. It don't take no more than fifty cents a day to feed the three of us. We's country folks. Glad to git cornbread and beans and potatoes and greens. I've heard some doctors say you could live on cornbread and vegetables without meat. I doubt it. Not and be hardy. I try to git meat for us at least twice a week. Fix an egg apiece for us at breakfast. I pay a nickel a day for a pint of milk for Cap. I know he ought to have it, a growing boy like he is. We never have had to spend a red cent on doctors' bills for no one of us. Not even when Cap come. It didn't cost me nothing because the midwife was a friend of mine. She wouldn't hear of me paying her for helping me through. . . .

Wanting a Better Life

Me and Calvin wasn't only thinking about easy going for our own selves when we come to Knoxville. We knowed Cap would have a better chance at schooling here. And do you know what? That boy ain't turned sixteen yet and here he wants to quit school and go to work. Some ways I don't blame him. As hard as we work it looks like it just never is anything left over for us to throw to him to spend for fun. And they ain't a soul lives around here I care for him to run with. Well, both me and Calvin carries burial insurance. It'll git us out of his way without cost if anything happens to us. I don't see no sense in paying out for that on Cap yet. He's not going to die no time soon. If he's going to start out for hisself, I want him to have some sort of a good job. He can have every penny he makes for hisself, too. I don't believe in milking your children.

I told him it's got to be some good straight job. Some boys git it in their heads that they can make a sight of money selling liquor. The law cracks down on them almost as soon as they git a start. We see it happen every day around here. You've got to keep the law paid off a good and plenty or else the penitentiary is where they's going to land. Now if they does pay off, where is the profit left from selling? Ain't none. So there they is. I told Cap if he had it in his head to do that, he better be clearing his head of it right now.

I don't blame him one bit for having his mind set on making a little money to have fun on. Seems like me and Calvin ain't never done a thing ever but work hard all our lives. Some folks find pleasure in going to meeting on Sunday. But it's no church I've had sight of here in Knoxville where the ones coming in and out ain't dressed up fit to kill. Some says it's all the same in the eyes of the Lord about how you dress. But I knows if He's got sense at all, He knows our clothes is too wore out for Sunday strutting. I know they's shabby in my own sight.

Calvin and me both can read right well. In times back we use to read the Bible pretty much. But seems like you always come across something you can't make out straight. So we just stopped reading it. Looked a pure shame, as wore out as we was, to read things that upset your head.

I guess I got on to the main of it, though. I know that Jesus Christ died to save sinners. And all that me and Calvin have to do is trust in Him. And we do. And we believe in Him. I don't see where they's any way to keep me and Calvin out of Heaven. Calvin moved away from the mountains to keep a killing from happening. That clears what's said about not killing. We ain't never stole and have always told the truth. We never brought false witness against nobody. They's more to it, but I counted them off one day and we is all right. Calvin and me ain't never harmed a living soul in our lives. So I ain't bothering about Hell if I never gits inside the door of a Knoxville church. When me and Calvin gits there I'd be more than glad to do what I could to help others git in.

They's some folks, not a thousand miles away from here, that are going to need a heap of helping. Ah, Lordy, yes!"

The Dust Bowl

Ann Marie Low

> During the Depression the Great Plains areas from Colorado
> to Kansas and the Oklahoma and Texas panhandles experi-
> enced severe drought that lasted for years. The regions
> became known as the dustbowl because of the dust storms
> that often blackened the skies. These storms were caused by
> overcultivation and poor land management during the twen-
> ties, which plowed over all of the native grasses that anchored
> the soil. The drought dried the earth and the winds blew all of
> the topsoil into the sky. Ann Marie Low lived with her family
> in the Great Plains of South Dakota during the Depression.
> The following excerpt includes stories taken from her diary.
> She describes how she and her family tried to keep their farm
> going despite the drought and the dust storms.

April 25, 1934, Wednesday: Last weekend was the worst
dust storm we ever had. We've been having quite a bit
of blowing dirt every year since the drought started, not only
here, but all over the Great Plains. Many days this spring the
air is just full of dirt coming, literally, for hundreds of miles.
It sifts into everything. After we wash the dishes and put
them away, so much dust sifts into the cupboards we must
wash them again before the next meal. Clothes in the clos-
ets are covered with dust.

Last weekend no one was taking an automobile out for
fear of ruining the motor. I rode Roany to Frank's place to
return a gear. To find my way I had to ride right beside the
fence, scarcely able to see from one fence post to the next.

Newspapers say the deaths of many babies and old people are attributed to breathing in so much dirt.

May 7, 1934, Monday: The dirt is still blowing. Last weekend [my brother] Bud and I helped with the cattle and had fun gathering weeds. Weeds give us greens for salad long before anything in the garden is ready. We use dandelions, lamb's quarter, and sheep sorrel. I like sheep sorrel best. Also, the leaves of sheep sorrel, pounded and boiled down to a paste, make a good salve.

Still no job. I'm trying to persuade Dad I should apply for rural school #3 out here where we went to school. I don't see a chance of getting a job in a high school when so many experienced teachers are out of work,

He argues that the pay is only $60.00 a month out here, while even in a grade school in town I might get $75.00. Extra expenses in town would probably eat up that extra $15.00. Miss Eston, the practice teaching supervisor, told me her salary has been cut to $75.00 after all the years she has been teaching in Jamestown. She wants to get married. School boards will not hire married women teachers in these hard times because they have husbands to support them. Her fiancé is the sole support of his widowed mother and can't support a wife, too. So she is just stuck in her job, hoping she won't get another salary cut because she can scarcely live on what she makes and dress the way she is expected to. . . .

I figure I can handle the work, kids, and patrons. My argument is that by teaching here I can work for my room and board at home, would not need new clothes, and so could send most of my pay to Ethel and Bud.

In April, Ethel had quit college, saying she did not feel well.

May 21, 1934, Monday: . . . Saturday Dad, Bud, and I planted an acre of potatoes. There was so much dirt in the air I couldn't see Bud only a few feet in front of me. Even the air in the house was just a haze. In the evening the wind died down, and [my boyfriend] Cap came to take me to the movie. We joked about how hard it is to get cleaned up enough to go anywhere.

The newspapers report that on May 10 there was such a

strong wind the experts in Chicago estimated 12,000,000 tons of Plains soil was dumped on that city. By the next day the sun was obscured in Washington, D.C., and ships 300 miles out at sea reported dust settling on their decks.

Sunday the dust wasn't so bad. Dad and I drove cattle to the Big Pasture. Then I churned butter and baked a ham, bread, and cookies for the men, as no telling when Mama will be back.

May 30, 1934, Wednesday: . . . The mess was incredible! Dirt had blown into the house all week and lay inches deep on everything. Every towel and curtain was just black. There wasn't a clean dish or cooking utensil. There was no food. Oh, there were eggs and milk and one loaf left of the bread I baked the weekend before. I looked in the cooler box down the well (our refrigerator) and found a little ham and butter. It was late, so Mama and I cooked some ham and eggs for the men's supper because that was all we could fix in a hurry. It turned out they had been living on ham and eggs for two days.

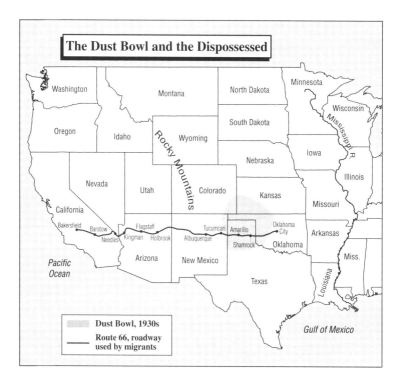

The Dust Bowl and the Dispossessed

Mama was very tired. After she had fixed starter for bread, I insisted she go to bed and I'd do all the dishes. . . .

It took until 10 o'clock to wash all the dirty dishes. That's not wiping them—just washing them. The cupboards had to be washed out to have a clean place to put them.

Saturday was a busy day. Before starting breakfast I had to sweep and wash all the dirt off the kitchen and dining room floors, wash the stove, pancake griddle, and dining room table and chairs. There was cooking, baking, and churning to be done for those hungry men. Dad is 6 feet 4 inches tall, with a big frame. Bud is 6 feet 3 inches and almost as big-boned as Dad. We say feeding them is like filling a silo.

Mama couldn't make bread until I carried water to wash the bread mixer. I couldn't churn until the churn was washed and scalded. We just couldn't do anything until something was washed first. Every room had to have dirt almost shoveled out of it before we could wash floors and furniture.

We had no time to wash clothes, but it was necessary. I had to wash out the boiler, wash tubs, and the washing machine before we could use them. Then every towel, curtain, piece of bedding, and garment had to be taken outdoors to have as much dust as possible shaken out before washing. The cistern is dry, so I had to carry all the water we needed from the well.

That evening Cap came to take me to the movie, as usual. . . . I'm sorry I snapped at Cap. It isn't his fault, or anyone's fault, but I was tired and cross. Life in what the newspapers call "the Dust Bowl" is becoming a gritty nightmare.

As commencement of June 6 approached, there was still no job in sight. Much as I wanted to get away, it seemed best to apply for no. 3, the rural school a mile and a half from home. The folks needed me. I could work for my room and board at home and have no extra clothes expense. The $60.00 a month would stretch over a lot of bills.

The school board was glad to hire me. By 1934 a rural school teacher had to be better educated than formerly, but

*still needed only one year of college. Since I had four, the
board thought that made me all the better teacher. They got*

Inside the Dust Storm

*The farmers that lived in the arid Panhandle not only had
to endure years of drought but also the many dust storms
that darkened the skies for miles. For those who chose to
stay with their farms, the sand became part of their everyday lives. Nathan Asch is an author who wrote about his
travels in Oklahoma during those dark days. The following is an excerpt from his book,* The Road.

It was in Oklahoma that I went inside the dust storm that
for three weeks obscured the sun and made everything,
food, water, even the air taken into the lungs, taste gritty.
It blew into the eyes, underneath the collar; undressing,
there were specks of dust inside the buttonholes; in the
morning it had gathered like fine snow along the window
ledge; it penetrated even more; it seeped along the wiring
of the house; and along the edges of the door button there
was a brown dusty stain. Sometimes it did not blow; it
stood between the buildings, dulling them, and dulling the
mind, making thoughts oppressive, giving the city a mood
of foggy melancholy. As in a disaster one only thought of
dust, one saw it, felt it, tasted it and lost his sense of smell.
In the country, the road, the ditches, the fields, the grass,
the plants, even the sky above, everything was covered by
the dust; cattle stood head down, immovable, not tasting
the gritty leaves; automobiles went slowly; and when even
the road was obscured from the driver's vision and all the
world, everything that one could possibly see was just a
brownness, one had to stop and wait.

Until I had gone over the crest of mountains in Wyoming,
the dust was always there. Everything I thought was com-
plicated by the thought of dust; in everything I ate I tasted
dust. It was the last thing before I fell asleep, and the first
thing with consciousness at waking.

Nathan Asch, *The Road*. New York: Norton, 1937.

stung. I was trained as a high school teacher and could teach upper grades but didn't know how to teach a first grader to read. The pay was actually $59.40, as 60¢ was taken out each month for retirement fund.

At home there was less work to do than usual. There had been no moisture since Easter. The crops which hadn't blown out had baked in the ground. There would be no grain to cut and shock. The garden never came up. There was no corn to cultivate; it had not come up either. The hay meadows were rapidly burning up in the hot sun.

But what would we live on? The poultry and cream checks would not be enough. The cattle were starving out. Dad and Grover [my uncle] had already shipped a carload for practically nothing, and more would have to go. We were pasturing them on what was left of the grain fields.

Dad's herd was being sacrificed for nothing. At a time of life when he should have been able to slow up, he was working harder than ever, getting less money than ever, and seeing his lifetime of work go down the drain.

Cap was feeling blue. He had the support of his stepmother and five half-sisters and brothers as well as his father's debts to pay. He could clear up the debts if he could get just one good crop. He had promised his stepmother he would stay and run the farm until his oldest half-brother was old enough. When that time came, the brother married and moved away to a rented place elsewhere. So it was necessary to wait until the next brother was old enough.

In late June I wrote:

One of the kittens fell down the well this morning. Bud and I nearly broke our necks getting him out in time to save a funeral in the family.

This country doesn't look pretty any more; it is too barren. I'm herding the milk cows on what is left of the grain fields. We replanted the corn and garden. Dad has the best well in this vicinity. If it holds out, we can carry water to the garden. If it doesn't rain, the corn is out of luck. . . .

July 6, 1934, Friday: I am still herding cows, and it is awfully hot. Where they have eaten every weed and blade of grain, Bud is plowing so the ground will be softened to absorb rain (if it comes). He is very fed up and anxious to get away to school and fit himself for a job.

Poor Bud. He has worked so hard and saved so hard. He has done without nice clothes and never went to a dance or movie oftener than about once a year because he was saving every penny for college. He hoped his livestock would pay his way for four years. The price was so low he didn't sell any last year. This year they are worth less, and he absolutely must sell them because there is not enough feed for them and no money to buy feed. All the stock he has won't pay his way through one year of college. . . .

July 9, 1934, Monday: Saturday night Cap and I went to the movie, Claudette Colbert in *The Torch Singer.* Afterward he bought ice cream cones and we sat in the car in front of the store eating them. He brought up the subject of marriage. I reminded him that he promised, if I would go out with him occasionally, he would not mention marriage. I also pointed out the impossibility. He has to run the farm until Sonny is old enough and then will have nothing to start out on his own. I have to work until Ethel gets through college and can help Bud, at least two years. If she doesn't help Bud, we are looking at four years. Though I didn't mention it, in four years Cap will be thirty-six years old. Forget it. . . .

July 18, 1934, Wednesday: It is 104° in the shade. The grain fields are all eaten up, so I'm herding the cows along the ditches of the roads. The garden is burned up. We don't dare carry water to it because the well is going dry and we need all the water there is for us and the livestock. The river is dry. We have fenced a lane from the Big Pasture to the lake so the beef cattle will have access to water.

August 1, 1934, Wednesday: Everything is just the same—hot and dry. Lee [Ferguson, a friend of the family] came from Medora for a visit. It was so nice to see him. He wants me to go out there Christmas vacation.

The drought and dust storms are something fierce. As far as one can see are brown pastures and fields which, in the wind, just rise up and fill the air with dirt. It tortures animals and humans, makes housekeeping an everlasting drudgery, and ruins machinery.

The crops are long since ruined. In the spring wheat section of the U.S., a crop of 12 million bushels is expected instead of the usual 170 million. We have had such drought for five years all subsoil moisture is gone. Fifteen feet down the ground is dry as dust. Trees ore dying by the thousands. Cattle and horses are dying, some from starvation and some from dirt they eat on the grass.

The government is buying cattle, paying $20.00 a head for cows and $4.00 for calves, and not buying enough to do much good.

Chapter 5

Taking It on the Road

Chapter Preface

During the Depression, millions of people took to the roads looking for jobs and adventure. They hitched rides, walked along highways, and hopped on freight trains that crisscrossed the country. A large number of hoboes during the Depression were not even adults. A quarter of a million of them were teenagers and children. Many communities that had burned through their budgets trying to provide relief to the needy were forced to shut down schools as a last resort. With no jobs available or schools to attend, many children left home so they wouldn't be a burden on their family. Others saw a good opportunity to run away from an abusive homelife. Many itinerants were also women, some of whom took their families on the road with them. The hobo life for single women could be dangerous, so many either disguised themselves by dressing in men's clothing or traveled in groups.

There is a lot of romance surrounding hobo culture. It's a unique lifestyle that has its own traditions, mythology, and community. But the public tended to lump all itinerants into one group. In reality there were different classes of itinerants. There were hoboes, who were migratory workers; tramps, who abhorred work; yeags, who were itinerant criminals; and bums, who tended to be shiftless alcoholics. All these people could be found in "jungles," which were itinerant communities that sprang up alongside train tracks and outside of towns. Many of the jungles were more than haphazard Hoovervilles. They often had rules and bosses who enforced them. "Jungle buzzards" were older, veteran hoboes who controlled who came in or out of the jungle. Anybody who wanted to stay had to talk with the jungle buzzard, who delegated chores to the newcomers. What seemed like a colorful life was in reality a difficult one filled with hunger and loneliness.

The Road Out of Town

Benjamin Appel

> As the Depression deepened, conditions seemed to get worse. Unemployment increased and houses and farms were being foreclosed at an alarming rate. Everybody seemed to be on the move looking for something better in the next town or the next state. Benjamin Appel was a writer who roamed around the country interviewing people from all walks of life. In the following excerpt he interviews A.C. Brown, the owner of a small garage in Oklahoma City, and Mercer, a tire shop owner. Both shops were the last stops out of town for many. Many of their customers could not afford to pay them.

Ramsey Tower is on North Robinson Avenue in the Oklahoma City of movies, restaurants and money-in-the bank business. But ten blocks south on Robinson Avenue, the eating joints offer: MEALS 15c, the rooming houses: Rooms 25c–50c. The stores attract the man with a hole in his pocket: MONEY FOR SMALL TOOLS. And further south, Robinson puts on four wheels and becomes one automobile supply store, catering to the man with the jaloppy.

NEAL SALVAGE

WE RENT TRAILERS

BUICK CAR $25.

Tire tubes hang on wooden elbows on both sides of South Robinson Avenue. Hub caps from Fords, Plymouths, Chryslers, shine in bright chromium rows outside the accessory stores. The sidewalks are unpaved as if no one ever walked much here, good enough sidewalks for a man who leaves his wheel only because he has to fix his car or buy a tire.

A.C. BROWN AUTO REPAIRS. The plate glass, lettered in red and white, is between two driveways, the shed-like structure a one-story corrugated tin building. Inside, there is no floor of stone or cement. The brown earth is packed hard like a country blacksmith's. A.C. Brown, a wiry man of about forty with sharply defined cheekbones and blue eyes, walks over to me, a pair of black acetylene glasses pushed up on his forehead.

"Who are your customers"? I ask him. "That is if you don't mind telling me. . ."

"I don't mind. The people that comes down here . . . there's a majority and a minority," he says in the low-pitched flat voice of middle America. "The majority are the extreme poor ones. They tell me people have less money every day. Wages're being cut, less people working. They come here from all sections of the country. You take myself. I come from Kansas and Nebraska. I been in business about six years and the last two years, business been gittin' worse and worse. Practically all the second-hand tires've been picked up." His eyes are deeply blue in the pallor of his expressionless face. Only his eyes glow with an intense effort to communicate what he's seen. "The people that comes down here are an American class of people, losin' their homes and possessions. It's very hard for them to buy a car even as low as twenty-five dollars. Some of 'em hike or buy a cheap Model T. That's all they have left. A lot of 'em come from Kansas, Nebrasky, Arkansas, Missouri, and quite a number from Texas. They hear about Oklahoma City. This is a cheap city to live in and it don't get too cold here. But when they get here, their li'l sum of money's spent. A lot of 'em end in Community Camp. That's their final graveyard."

Kansas, Nebraska, Arkansas, Missouri, the core of the American continent; freezing Kansas, the geographical center of the forty-eight states. . . . And Oklahoma just to the south of Kansas. Highway 62 into Oklahoma City. Highway 66 into Oklahoma City. Highway 77 into Oklahoma City. Highway 270 into Oklahoma City. Highway 277 into Oklahoma City.

Hike or Ride, They're Always Going Out

"A lot of the people hikes out. But if they get where they want to go . . . that's just a chance. Some gets there and some don't. What I'm in, is garage and weldin'. The people're not gettin' work and that's squashin' the middle businessman out of existence. They buy an old jaloppy. They'll run from five to fifteen dollars. A Ford or a Chevy'll run from thirty to fifty. . . . I'd hate like hell to start out myself in one of 'em. They start all right, but how far do they go?" His voice never rises, flat as the plains. "But you'll find in each family, one who'll know how to keep the motor goin'. Some one in the family's skilled. Generally, they'll do their own work if they can. There was a car, an old Buick come in here, a father and a mother and six children from Arkansas. They lost their home. It was a li'l eighty-acre farm. They said they only got three hundred out of eighty acres. We tightened the rods and

Auto shop and garage owners in many small towns witnessed hundreds of people passing by on their way out of town.

made brake adjustments and weldin' on the fenders. The job come to five dollars. We fixed it up the best we could and they only had three dollars. Some people can't pay nothing and give a wheel for payment. . . . All the time we was weldin' the Buick they hung around. They had their personal belongings in the car. It was a '25 or '26 Buick. They said they were going to try to get work here. I don't know what happened to them. I judge the father was about fifty-three or fifty-four. A family'll head west for Californy until they find work. . . . There was a man and a woman and a girl, eight years old. They had an Oldsmobile. They traded their chickens for five gallons of gas. He harvested in Nebraska. We fixed his car. He said he wanted work. He ast here about work. He had his beddin' and dishes in the back and the three of 'em were sittin' in front."

The sign on the wall reads: IT'S HELL TO BE A CRIPPLE. BE CAREFULL.

"I used to farm. . . . My brothers're having a hell of a struggle."

Up and down on South Robinson Avenue, the cars, the cars, the cars, the new cars, the old cars, the old cars, the old cars, the old cars. . . .

Eight Hundred Tires

Across the traffic. I enter Mercer's tire shop. Mercer, himself, a young man in overalls and cap, glances up from the tire he is repairing, strips of raw black rubber in his hands. Deftly, he pastes a strip down upon the patched-up hole.

"How many tires have you got?"

"I have about six hundred or eight hundred tars," he answers. "Every time a fillin' station moves or goes bankrupt, I buy a lot of tars. Do you want one?"

"No. I just want to talk about tires."

He smiles, pastes in a second rubber strip. "We got two hundred and fifty second-hand tar shops for vulcanizin' and retreadin' here. I handle a cheap grade. I sell for seventy-five cents to a dollar. I sell my share." His tiny shop is one wheel of tires, tires with jagged cuts, tires with patches, tires with boots, old tires, worn tires. In the yard to the rear of the store, hundreds of tires fill up the wooden tireholders.

"Who do you sell to?"

"I have a lot of transits goin' to Arizony, New Mexico and California. I got an uncle in Madera right now. There's five of 'em and they're pickin' grapes and cotton. My aunt, she's sick. The others are all right." He works rapidly. "I had one transit back from Arizony. He was from Oklahoma. He was gittin' sixty-five cents a hundred pounds pickin' cotton, bumblebee cotton. That's hard to pick. A dollar and a half was all he could pick in a day. I fixed his tube for a quarter and sold him a tar for fifty cents. He had about fifteen, twenty dollars. Just enough to live on two weeks or a month."

The Tire Business

"You always live here?"

"I was born in Oklahoma and went to Virginia. But I've lived here ever since '21 before the flood. I quit school when I was in the tenth grade. When I was eighteen I got married. I'm married four years and I've been in this business about six. To make money a feller has to work twelve, fourteen hours a day. Most of 'em in the tar business make a poor livin'." He slaps the tire he is repairing. "This tar cost me two bits and I'll sell it for a dollar. I don't guarantee these. These transits . . . nine-tenths of 'em want a tar for a dollar, to two and a half, and a new tread." He begins to repair another torn tire. "I'd get twice as much out of a tar five years ago than I could get now. In the last year, to year and a half, old tars've gone up two hundred per cent Times is gittin' harder. I'm buyin' tars at two bits a piece but two years from now, I'll pay six bits. People're holdin' on to their tars. Good tars with a small hole is seldom to be found. Now they'll keep it and stick a boot in. Not all my customers is transits. I got customers who work for the companies here in town. The man with a good income, ***** to twenty-five a week job, he'll pay two, three dollars for a tar and not cry.

He stares up at me. "As for transits, there's two kinds. The people who git a paid vacation and those flat broke. There's a transit who foller the Government jobs, the Boulder Dam. There's transits who go to New Mexico and Arizony to pick cotton. There's the young fellers who go out to Californy and come back broke in thirty days to six months. I had a brother who went out to Bakersfield, drivin' an oil field truck. He come back in six months. I stay here and watch them transits. I pay ten dollars a month rent. And I'm not makin' a poor livin' neither." He straightens his back, smiles. "I don't mind workin' twelve to fourteen hours a day."

Outside on South Robinson Avenue, I look straight north to Ramsey Tower, the First National skyscraper alongside. Twinned, they stand in the blue sky as if standing in another city, in another time.

Riding the Rails

John Fawcett

> During the Depression, slashed educational budgets forced
> schools to be downsized or closed. With few jobs available, the
> opportunities for young people were limited. Many teenagers
> and children left home so they wouldn't be a burden on their
> families. They hopped on freight trains or hitchhiked, moving
> aimlessly from one end of the country to the other. They
> worked odd jobs and sent what money they could spare back
> home. Others left home mainly for the adventure. In 1936 John
> Fawcett was sixteen when he left home to ride the rails. He'd
> had enough of the military school his father had sent him to in
> 1936 and yearned for adventure. But the thrills he found were
> always tempered by the harsh reality of hoboing. Recorded
> here by Errol Lincoln Uys, Fawcett's accounts of jail and
> scraping by for food were common among young hoboes.

I hardly knew there was such a thing as the Great Depression, because we never had it hard. At Christmas my mom would take us kids down to a local settlement house with baskets of food for the poor and their families. My dad [an ophthalmologist] would send my older brother to do collections for overdue fees on Saturdays. Other than that, I'd no idea of what was going on in the country. We still had two automobiles. We went on summer vacations to the eastern shore of Maryland. We lived the good life.

I went to public school for four years. Then my dad sent my two brothers and me to military college. That's where he and his brother went. Fawcett boys attended Linsly and that

Excerpted from John Fawcett's account in *Riding the Rails: Teenagers on the Move During the Great Depression,* edited by Errol Lincoln Uys. Copyright © 1999 by Errol Lincoln Uys. Reprinted with permission from TV Books.

was that. We got to wear a uniform, which was a big thing for the first year. Afterwards it got to be a bloody nuisance. By the time I reached high school, I hated the discipline.

Mom and Dad were good, loving parents, so I certainly didn't run away because of my home life. Why do boys run away? For adventure, I guess, because it's exciting and dangerous.

I ran away from home three different times. I always left a note on my dad's desk, telling him not to worry. I can only imagine what my mother felt.

At about eleven o'clock that February night, I walked into the waiting room of the B&O [Baltimore and Ohio Railroad] passenger station. I walked onto the lighted platform, where people were standing around, and sauntered toward the front of Train Number 77. It originated in Pittsburgh and made a stop at Wheeling, then followed the Ohio River south to Huntington, West Virginia, 180 miles distant. I had a friend who'd moved to Huntington the year before and wanted to visit him. Beyond that, I'd no idea where I would go or what I would do.

I took a quick look at the blind behind the engine tender of Number 77. It would be an easy place to ride, with my back against the baggage car door.

I walked about fifty feet ahead of the engine and ducked behind a small building. I could see the railroad tracks in the glare of the locomotive headlight. I heard a hoot from the engine whistle and saw her big driving wheels begin to turn.

As the huge locomotive chuffed past me, I stepped from my shelter onto the snow-covered roadbed. I caught the grab-iron on the back of the tender with my gloved hand. My foot was in the stirrup and I was on my way!"

A Short Trip to Jail

John's weekend dash for freedom ended at Huntington, when his friend's parents contacted the Fawcetts and arranged for him to be shipped home "riding the cushions." In June 1936, when John and his friend Mick McKinley, fifteen, ran away, they planned to ride the rails to the Texas Centennial Expo-

sition and afterwards find work as cowboys.

Around midnight our train pulled into the big passenger station in Parkersburg, West Virginia. The train hadn't stopped, and there was a gun and a flashlight in my face. A B&O bull [railroad police] told us to climb down, took us one on each arm, and marched us down the platform, between the people getting on and off the train. I don't ever remember being so humiliated. The bull took us to the Wood County Jail. In ten minutes, we were behind bars.

My first impression was the awful stink of confined humanity and stale urine. I hadn't known what the inside of a jail was like, but sure found out over the next four days. We had a cell mate, Nick, a petty thief who had a good deal of street sense. He warned us to keep our mouths shut and not smart off to anybody. He told us about "the Brute," a prisoner who ran the jail. "He holds the kangaroo court," said our cell mate. The kangaroo court was an informal procedure run by the inmates, the Brute acting as judge. "He'll have you over to his cell tomorrow."

At 7:30 A.M., a guard did the rounds with a kitchen worker, bringing a cart with breakfast. "Dreadful" is the best word I can think of for the food: a bowl of cold oatmeal, a slice of bread, a cup of bitter black fluid, which Nick told us was chicory. At noon, we would be fed lukewarm, tasteless soup; another slice of bread; and a cup of chicory. The evening's fare was a half stew—half soup "slumgullion," as Nick called it.

At ten o'clock that morning, the Brute's henchman came across the bullpen. "You take any money from these kids?" he asked Nick, who replied respectfully, "No, Sir." The pug looked at Mick. "He get anything from you guys?" Mick's response was, "We didn't have nuthin' to take." With a surly look at both of us, he said, "We'll see about that. Kangaroo court is on. Come with me."

The Brute was sitting on a wooden chair in his cell. Nick had told us that he was doing a year in jail for killing a man in a barroom brawl.

"How much money did the jailer get from you last

night?" the Brute asked. The jailer-judge who admitted us had "fined" us ten dollars or ten days in jail. Mick and I had each produced three dollars and were told we would have to serve out the rest of our fine.

"How much you got left?" asked the Brute.

"Three dollars," I replied.

He asked Mick. "A dollar, maybe more," he said.

"Take off your shoes and let's have it."

What a deflating experience! Mick and I had thought we were so damned clever hiding stuff in our shoes. The kangaroo court took all the money I had left: $3.79. There was yet one brief scene to play out. The Brute told us to strip to prove we had no money belts. Satisfied we had nothing more, they dismissed us and sent us back to our cells.

Sunday evening brought an experience that lowered my spirits even further. About 7:30, the guards admitted eight or ten evangelistic church folk, who sang and prayed and extolled us to salvation before the fires of hell consumed us. I didn't need that. I just wanted something to eat.

Mick and I were in our cell on Tuesday afternoon when we heard the now-familiar clang of jail doors opening and closing. A voice reverberated through the hallway: "Kendall and Murphy coming out!"

We were lying on our bunks in silence, until Mick suddenly yelled, "John, that's us!" We'd agreed on using assumed names on the trip in case we ran into the law.

We identified ourselves and were told we were to be released.

Let out that afternoon, Mick and I both had fair success in knocking at doors and asking for food. Mick was the winner, bringing a chunk of sausage wrapped in a piece of oily newspaper. We went down to the west end of the B&O freight yards. A crossing guard pointed out the next train to Cincinnati. It was a hotshot, a fast freight, which we caught, reclining on the top of a boxcar as the train rumbled over the Ohio River. Mick and I smiled and shook hands, hearing the bark from the exhaust stacks and the wail of the steam whistle. We were free of the confines of Wood County Jail.

Lost in the Freight Yard

That evening I learned one thing for certain. When you are on the road away from friends and home, it is comforting and reassuring to be acknowledged and recognized by people along the way—strangers though they may be. I saw people wave at us from their fields and from their porches and backyards as we went rattling past. There were so many unemployed and destitute people that I think they felt a kinship.

We arrived at Chillicothe, Ohio, about midnight. At the large freight yard, we saw several figures in the dark, carrying flashlights or lanterns. Mick and I had met two West Virginia lads on the freight. We started running around the cars to avoid getting caught and lost Mick in the dark. The two lads and I spent an hour looking for him. It didn't seem like a good idea to go around calling his name, so we gave up. We found an unlocked caboose on a side track and spent a comfortable night inside, sleeping on the bunks.

A young girl carrying supplies walks toward the railroad car that is her home. During the Depression, many young people traveled across the country in train boxcars.

The sun was up when we rolled out and started walking up a street away from the yards. We'd gone a couple of blocks when I saw two railroad men coming toward us.

Walking beside them, smiling and talking jovially, was old Mick McKinley, who greeted us nonchalantly as you please. The railroad men invited all of us to coffee and pancakes!

We loafed around the Chillicothe yards for a couple of hours before a B&O fast freight came storming out of the yards. We leaped aboard and climbed to the top for a scenic ride in the morning sunshine. Later, we arrived at the Mill Creek marshaling yards at Cincinnati. We'd lucked out again.

Working for Food

We walked to an area close to the yards and spent an hour or two on what would become a never-ending quest for "a little work in exchange for something to eat." You always hoped a woman would answer the door, as women were more sympathetic to someone in bad straits.

It's hard at first for a sixteen-year-old to ask for food, especially coming from the perfectly safe environment that I'd always known. But you learn it in a bloody hurry, when you're hungry and haven't eaten for twenty-four or thirty-six hours. I never learned to panhandle—it was better to offer to work. "Is there something I can do? Got any errands? Chop some wood?" You don't feel that you're getting something for nothing. That's the way I justified it. Probably half the time you made that offer there was no work, but you got something to eat anyway.

Later, we learned how to "put the bum" on restaurants. You walk back and forth in front of a restaurant and look for a man on a stool at a counter. Preferably, two men with an empty stool in between. You buzz right in there, plop down next to them, and speak right up to the waitress. "Have you got any work to do? I haven't eaten since the day before yesterday."

Sometimes a waitress would slip a cup of coffee in front of you. The kicker is that if you get turned down, there's a good chance one of the people beside you will pipe up and say, "It's OK lady, give the man his breakfast. I'll pay for it." And then you're home free. It got easier every time. You knew what to say and not to be crushed if you were refused.

Another way to get food was bumming bakeries for two- or three-day-old dinner rolls or doughnuts called "toppings." You get a sack of toppings and you've got a meal—not a balanced meal, but it lasts you for a few hours.

I never felt I was treated with disgust by people when I put the bum on them. Sympathy, pity maybe, but never "Why don't you go to work?" Everybody in the country knew there was no damn work.

Rules of the Jungle

Some nights on the road, we slept in boxcars. It's quick and easy to find an empty boxcar in a railroad yard. Some nights we spent in hobo jungles [hobo encampment]. There'd often be old jungle buzzards, who lived there for weeks or months at a time. You'd ask permission if you wanted to do something: "Hey, I want to wash my clothes. Is that OK?" And the 'bo would say, "Yeah, well, go downtown and bring us back some cabbage and you can do whatever you want."

I remember sitting around the jungles sometimes all day long. When you missed a train there wasn't another until that night. Most of the people we saw were in their twenties and thirties, some older than that. There were probably more women than we recognized, because they didn't wear women's clothes. We saw Okie families dispossessed from their farms heading west to California. Some were awful looking, in real terrible condition, and dreadfully near starvation. Many lacked the courage to go up to somebody and ask for something.

Every freight train had dozens, sometimes hundreds of people on the cars. It didn't matter which direction the train was traveling, it would be loaded with guys going east and going west and going south. "No use going back East to Minneapolis. I just came from there and there's nothing," a guy would say in the jungle. When the train came, people would get on and go to Minneapolis anyway. Anything was better than sitting in the jungle, complaining and getting hungry.

People usually referred to us as "kid"—"Hey, kid, get moving there; you're going to get your leg cut off;" "Hey, kid, chop some wood for the fire." They called us kids and that's what we were. It didn't bother us. I think it made it easier, not rougher, because people respond to young children. We took advantage of that.

This is not to romanticize being on the road. Riding the blinds of a speeding passenger train is the quickest way to get killed in the world aside from being a fighter pilot. It is awful and dangerous. I was hungry all the time and I wasn't used to hunger. Sometimes two to three days without anything to eat. When you're active and moving, your hunger hurts physically.

Listening to Townsfolk

John and Mick rode freight trains from Cincinnati southwest to Gosport, Indiana, where Mick met a young man whose father offered him a few days' work. The same individual told the boys his uncle owned a sawmill in Marshall, Arkansas, where they could find summer jobs. Their plan to attend the Texas Centennial Exposition temporarily shelved, John rode on ahead to Marshall. Only a week after leaving home, he crossed the Mississippi River at Thebes, Illinois. He made his way into Arkansas on the Missouri Pacific Railroad. He remembered the night he arrived at Little Rock, Arkansas, the night Joe Louis became heavyweight champion of the world. The next day, John traveled to Marshall, Arkansas.

Marshall was a small Ozark mountain town with a population of maybe a thousand. A typical small American country town. A block away and you're out in the country again.

I checked at the post office, the general store, and the barbershop. No one had ever heard of a sawmill near Marshall. There was nothing for me to do but to wait until Mick arrived.

My next move was to "apply for employment" at the barbershop. The barber was a kind old gent who gave me a dime for sweeping out the place. I spent my wages on a generous bowl of chili and crackers. After dark, I walked down to the railroad station, where I found an old baggage wagon. I climbed onto it and curled up for the night.

The romance of adventure was rapidly dwindling. I didn't like being all alone out in the country. When I was with other people on the trains or in the jungles, I didn't feel lonely or threatened. I felt excited at being part of something unique, even frightening, that was taking place in our country. What

---

Swallowed Up by the Streets

Of the million and a half men and women who wandered around the country during the Depression, over a quarter of a million of them were teenagers. With schools closing and no jobs available there was very little incentive to stay home, especially when both parents were out of work and unable to offer regular meals. The following excerpt is taken from a journal of Robert Carter as quoted in Milton Meltzer's Brother Can You Spare a Dime? *Carter was a young runaway who crisscrossed the country by hopping freight trains.*

Grabbed a freight towards Macon. Boys were scattered all over the train, with fifteen or twenty in the boxcar I was in. Some lay sleeping on old paper, others swapped yarns, passed on recipes, told each other of bad detectives, of good places and friendly people, and where to catch the trains in and out of big towns. One, a boy of twenty, was just off the chain gang [prison work crew] and showed us his leg raw from the shackles. . . .

Macon, Ga. We descended on Macon in a horde and were swallowed up by the streets. Yet we were there, dozens of us, bumming the same houses and restaurants, wandering the same streets, vague and lonely, ever on the move.

That night I slept in the Salvation Army. It was crowded with boys and young men, some with small grips, others with nothing but the shirts on their backs. One boy, a nightmare of rags and dirt, was so thin and far-gone that we tramps, ourselves destitute, gave him of our stock of goods.

Milton Meltzer, *Brother Can You Spare a Dime?: The Great Depression 1929–1933.* New York: Alfred A. Knopf, 1969.

I was experiencing was the human tragedy of the Great Depression, of which I'd learned practically nothing at home.

The next morning I circled the town to see if I'd missed anything. What I really needed was to be around people. I spent that hot summer's day hanging around the town square. At any given time, twenty to forty men, singly or in small groups, sat on their haunches or stood with their backs against the buildings, quietly talking or just putting in time. Most wore faded overalls and bore the dry, wizened look of men who spent their lives on hard-scrabble farms.

I listened to people on the real edge of grievous poverty and unemployment, talking about how tough life was. They weren't seeking sympathy. They were just talking to each other, sharing their ideas. There seemed to be a quiet desperation in their concern for the future.

Once or twice during the day, I was included in a conversation. "Where are you from, kid?" When they found out I was wandering around the country, they asked me what things were like on the road. "Are the folks in the cities as bad off as we hear tell?"

I was hearing about conditions in the country from the people themselves, not from the guys disconnected from society like hoboes. These people lived in one place and had homes and children; they were talking about the way things are. This made more impression on me than anything else on that trip.

A man in the square suggested that I go to a camp meeting at a local church—they served cookies and lemonade. The church was a block away and easy to find from the hymn-singing and hallelujahs. I walked in and sat near the back. A girl about my age in a print dress came down the aisle and got right down on her knees facing me. I felt horribly embarrassed and self-conscious and, seeing no tables of food, I left as soon as I could.

Back on Board

It was beginning to rain as I walked down to the railway station. I found shelter on the old baggage wagon, which stood under an overhanging roof. I remember hearing the rain on the roof and being in a quandary of despair that so much was going on in life that I'd never learned about at home or in school.

It was still raining when I woke in the morning and pulled on my shoes, my hat, and my jacket. I stood awhile under the roof with my hands in my pockets, looking down the tracks and feeling sorry for myself. Mick might never come, and it's a cinch I'd starve if I stayed here. I decided I must leave Marshall and go to Texas alone.

Just then I heard a locomotive whistle echoing through the Ozark hills. My transportation was on its way! It seemed ages before the engine finally came chuffing out of the woods. Four cars back, a boxcar moved slowly toward me with a tattered gangly hobo hanging from the ladder, ready to hit the ground. It was none other than young Mick McKinley.

Standing in the rain, it took less than a minute to convince Mick that there was no sawmill and no jobs. This was starvation city and we must get right back on the train and keep moving. And we did.

At Eureka Springs, Arkansas, we caught a westbound freight, climbing into a boxcar with fifteen to twenty people, including an Okie family with a baby that cried all the time. Hours passed before we clanked to a stop in the yards at Seligman, Missouri. A fellow went with the family to try and find a doctor for the child.

The same guy was in our car at 2 A.M., when we caught a freight headed for Fayetteville. The baby had diphtheria and had been taken to a hospital. There was much concern among those of us who'd been in the same boxcar. "Ain't a helluva lot we can do about it now," said the man. We all lay down to sleep as we rattled along in the dark.

A Day at the Fair

When John and Mick reached Dennison, Texas, the two boys went uptown to beg for food. They became separated and wouldn't see each other again until they were back in West Virginia. After looking unsuccessfully for Mick in the Dennison yards, John hopped a passenger train and rode the

blinds to Dallas. He arrived at 6:30 on a Sunday morning.
He walked out to the centennial fair and climbed a chain-
link fence to get inside the grounds.

I remember a feeling of exultation: "By God, I did it!"
After three hard weeks of beating the road, I'd reached the
fair. Hunger, however, spoiled my visit. I had one hot dog
all day, wolfing it down and feeling hungrier than before.

By the time I'd seen the fair, all I wanted to do was to go
home and get my feet under the dinner table again. Having
witnessed the masses wandering the country, I finally realized that finding jobs as cowboys—or any other kind of
work—was an impossible dream.

I sat on a bench at a bus stop in downtown Dallas. I had
blank paper and an envelope that a lady had given me in
Poteau a few days before. I wrote a letter to my mother
telling her I was on my way home.

That evening, I walked over to the freight yards and
caught a train to Greenville. I jumped off and got a timetable
at the station. The "Katy Flyer" was due out of Greenville
in an hour.

I waited at a lighted intersection. The barrier gates came
down, with blinking red lights and ringing bell. I could see
the engine of the Katy Flyer a hundred yards away. As the
locomotive came by, I ran inside the crossing gates. I
leaped for the ladder and swung up into the second blind.
Homeward bound!

That was the longest ride I would ever have on the blinds
of a passenger train: seven hours and 280 miles, as the Katy
Flyer made its dash up into northeastern Oklahoma. It
wasn't my hunger but the fear of falling asleep and tumbling
between the cars that was my biggest problem. I stood up
most of that long night in order to stay awake.

I was detected after daylight, just as the train was pulling
out of Muskogee, Oklahoma. Suddenly, the door of the baggage car swung wide open. A surprised U.S. Mail agent
stood looking down at me. It took him about one-tenth of a
second to unlimber his .45 [automatic pistol] and push it
right in my teeth.

"Outta here, 'bo. Hit the dirt. Now!"

I stepped quickly to the corner of the car, grabbed the handrail, and swung down. Minutes later, I was standing on a street in Muskogee. I felt faint from hunger and lack of sleep. I walked aimlessly along, until I saw a pawn shop and went inside.

I took my goggles out of my jacket pocket and laid them on the counter in front of an old man. I made a pitiful appeal, saying that I was trying to get home and hadn't eaten for two days. What would he give me for my goggles? I wore the goggles when riding the tops or in the blinds, but needed food more than protection from cinders.

The pawnbroker took the goggles, turned them over slowly in his hand. "I know times are hard, young man, but I can't give you more than twenty cents."

I could've jumped over the counter and hugged him, but I just said, "Yeah, well, that's OK." I took the two dimes and scurried out the door.

Within minutes, I was in a café spending my twenty cents on ham and eggs, potatoes, toast, and coffee! I can still see half a dozen meals I had on that trip, because of what they meant to me at the time. That breakfast in Muskogee stands above them all because of its life-restoring quality. After eating, I found an empty boxcar just beyond the station, crawled in, and fell asleep as soon as my head touched the floor.

About noon, I awoke to hear two switchmen arguing about the Yankees and Dodgers. An hour later, we were rattling through the Oklahoma countryside, arriving in Parsons, Kansas, about four that afternoon. I walked up the main street and bummed a sitdown meal at a café plus a sack of Bull Durham. Two meals and tobacco in one day. This was more like it!

In another hour, I was on a fast freight bound for Kansas City, where we arrived at one in the morning. At daylight, I walked across the Missouri River bridge to the Argentine yards. I was sitting on a pile of railroad ties, meditating on life, when an old gent came sauntering up to me. He had a bindle on his back and looked the part so I knew he was a brother of the road. We talked awhile, before he said he was going to buy lunch. Did I want to come along? I said that I was "on the nut," meaning that I'd no money.

"That's OK, kid. I'll spring this time."

That afternoon, my generous friend and I caught a freight headed east across central Missouri to Moberly. We arrived at six in the evening and went out on the town. I walked along the streets in a residential area a few blocks from the tracks. Looking in the window of one house, I saw a man sitting in his armchair reading the evening paper, and a couple of kids playing on the floor. I thought of my parents worrying about me.

It was getting dark when I went to look for my traveling partner, but didn't find him. A big locomotive came snorting by, leading a string of boxcars, and I climbed aboard.

The next day, I reached Decatur, where I grabbed a B&O hot shot headed east. It was a long ride but I had the satisfaction of being headed in the right direction. In the Indianapolis yards, the sun was well up when I boarded a Pennsylvania train, but I was kicked off in the little jerkwater town of Bradford, Ohio. I went out on the highway and hitchhiked into Springfield. I'd been twenty-four hours without food and was glad to score dinner at a restaurant. I found a jungle under an overpass east of the freight yards. Three or four guys were lying on the ground with newspapers wrapped around their bodies. I followed their example, and collecting some "Hoover blankets" [newspapers named after President Hoover, who was thought not to have done enough to help alleviate the Depression], I managed to get a fair night's sleep.

Pared Down to Ring Weight

I was 130 miles from home. I was homesick as hell! I finally leaped up onto a freight train around four o'clock in the afternoon.

On through the night, we charged through the hills of eastern Ohio. No fear of my sleeping that night! At two o'clock in the morning we rumbled slowly across the Ohio River bridge to the Benwood yards at Wheeling.

I got in stride for the seven-mile hike to my home in Woodsdale. When I finally stepped up onto the front porch, I lay down in our squeaky old glider swing and fell asleep.

Mary, a maid who'd been with our family for years, came downstairs to begin her daily routine. That Fourth of July morning in 1936, Mary got one helluva shock. Her yell woke me, as she leaned down to pick up the paper and saw a soot-covered fellow lying on the swing.

Mary went upstairs to Mother. "You'd better come down and see who's here to see you," she said. She told Mother that she didn't recognize me until I smiled.

After my dad got up and shaved, he came to me. He put out his hand and said, "Well, son, you're kinda down to ring weight, aren't you?"

That's all my dad said, and I loved him for it. My parents never gave me hell. Maybe they should have, I don't know, but that wouldn't have changed me.

A phone call to the McKinleys revealed that Mick had gotten back the day before. Fate had been kind to us both.

Sister of the Road

Box-Car Bertha

> Of the millions of people riding the rails during the thirties, many of them were young women. They often dressed in men's clothing and cut their hair to protect themselves. Many traveled singly while others traveled in groups for protection. Their reasons for leaving home were the same as for their male counterparts. They left for economic reasons or to find adventure. Box-Car Bertha is one of the most well known hobos and had ridden the rails most of her life. The following excerpt is from her book *Sister of the Road,* which was written by Ben L. Reitman. She discusses the different types of women she has encountered and the methods they used to get food, shelter, and protection.

Girls and women of every variety seemed to keep Chicago as their hobo center. They came in bronzed from hitch-hiking, in khaki. They came in ragged in men's overalls, having ridden freights, decking [riding on top] mail trains, riding the reefers [refrigerator cars], or riding the blinds on passenger trains. They came in driving their own dilapidated Fords or in the rattling side-cars of men hoboes' motorcycles. A few of them even had bicycles. They were from the west, south, east and north, even from Canada. They all centered about the Near North Side, in Bughouse Square, in the cheap rooming houses and light housekeeping establishments, or begged or accepted sleeping space from men or other women there before them. Some of them had paid their own way on buses or passenger trains but ar-

Excerpted from *Sister of the Road: The Autobiography of Box-Car Bertha,* as told to Ben L. Reitman. Copyright © 2000 by AK Press/Nabat, San Francisco & Edinburgh. Reprinted with permission from the AK Press.

rived broke to panhandle their food or berths with men temporarily able to keep them. A few had been stowaways on Lake boats, and I remember one who said she stowed away on an airplane from Philadelphia. Not a few of them had their ways paid by charity organizations believing their stories that they had relatives here who would keep them.

On arrival most of them were bedraggled, dirty, and hungry. Half of them were ill. There were pitiful older ones who had been riding freights all over the country with raging toothaches. In Chicago they got themselves to clinics, and although they couldn't get any dental work done free they could usually get the old snags of teeth taken out. Some were obviously diseased, and most of them were careless about their ailments unless they had overwhelming pain.

The bulk of these women, and most all women on the road, I should say, traveled in pairs, either with a man to whom by feeling or by chance they had attached themselves, or with another woman. A few had husbands and children with them. There were a number traveling with brothers. Now and then there was a group of college girls. A few women traveled about with a mob or gang of men. These were of the hard-boiled, bossy type, usually, who had careless sex relations with anyone in their own group, and who, therefore, never had to bother to hunt for food or shelter. I do not remember, during the first years, seeing many pairs of lesbians come in off the road together, but of course they are common now, women who are emotionally attached to each other, even though, on the road, or while they stop, they give their sex to men or to other women in exchange for food, transportation, and lodging.

The Types of Hobo Women

These women were out of every conceivable type of home. But even that first summer I could see what I know now after many years, that the women who take to the road are mainly those who come from broken homes, homes where the father and mother are divorced, where there are step-mothers or step-fathers, where both parents are dead, where they have had to live with aunts and uncles and grandparents. At least half the women on the road are out of such homes.

Many others, I have found, are graduates of orphan asylums. Shut up and held away from all activity, such girls have dreamed all their childhoods about traveling and seeing the world. As soon as they are released they take the quickest way to realizing their dreams, and become hoboes. Not a few are out of jails and institutions, choosing the road for freedom, the same way, regardless of hardship. Among these are actually many paroled from institutions for the feeble-minded and insane.

Managing Without Money

During my years in and out of Chicago I talked to hundreds of these women. How they managed without money on the road always fascinated me. Many worked from time to time. Some were typists, some file clerks, and carried with them recommendations from companies they had worked for. I knew one that first summer who was a graduate nurse. The only thing she carried with her on the road was a conservative looking dress which she could put on when she wanted to register for a job. She'd stay on a case, or a couple of cases, until she got a little money again, and then she'd pack the good dress away and go out on the road in trousers, hitch-hiking.

The bulk of the women on the road made no pretense of working, however, even when they stayed for weeks or even months, as they do in Chicago or any other big center. I have already explained how they get by, by begging, stealing or hustling, or with help from the welfare agencies.

Today, of course, all over the country there are state relief stations, federal transient bureaus, travelers' aid offices, but in the earlier days the missions and the private charities would help transients, especially women. Some of the girls made a specialty of all the words and attitudes that went with "being saved," and used them all successfully to get the watery soup and the coffee and bread that were put out by rescue missions in the name of the Lord. Some of them made up circumstantial stories of their Jewish ancestry (being Irish) and got emergency help from Jewish agencies. Or they manufactured Roman Catholic backgrounds (being Jewish) and got help from Catholic missions. Others had acquired the language of various lodges and fraternal organizations and in the name of fathers and brothers and uncles who were Masons, Moose, Woodmen, Kiwanians, they were given food or clothes or money for transportation.

But the great group of hobo women practiced none of these tricks. Most of them weren't clever enough. Instead they begged from stores and restaurants, from people on the road or on the city sidewalks. A lot of them didn't bother to beg rooms. If the weather was good they slept in the parks with the men, or alongside them, cleaning up in the morning in the toilets of the libraries or other public buildings. And on the Near North Side there were dozens of people in studios and rooming houses who would let any of them in for a bath or clean-up.

Life in the Jungles

Eric Sevareid

Hobos and tramps could be found congregated together alongside railroad tracks in encampments nicknamed "jungles."
These communities provided food, shelter, and company but
required newcomers perform chores—like begging food from
the local town—to be admitted. At night stories would be
exchanged around the campfire. Eric Sevareid was a writer
who grew up in Velva, North Dakota. As a teen he rode the
rails and passed through many jungles during his travels. In
the following excerpt from his autobiography, he discusses the
jungles and the dangers he encountered on the trains. Eric
Sevareid later became a respected journalist and author.

I awoke before dawn from a bed among the damp weeds by
the Union Pacific tracks at Sparks, the division point near
Reno [Nevada], and found an "empty" in the long freight train
making up for the thirty-six-hour run across the Great American Desert to Salt Lake. I entered a new social dimension, the
great underground world, peopled by tens of thousands of
American men, women, and children, white, black, brown,
and yellow, who inhabit the "jungle," eat from blackened tin
cans, find warmth at night in the box cars, take the sun by day
on the flatcars, steal one day, beg with cap in hand the next,
fight with fists and often razors, hold sexual intercourse under
a blanket in a dark corner of the crowded car, coagulate into
pairs and gangs, then disintegrate again, wander from town to
town, anxious for the next place, tired of it in a day, fretting to
be gone again, happy only when the wheels are clicking un-

der them, the telephone poles slipping by. Some were in honest search of work, but many were not. They had worked—once—but jobs did not last, pay was low, they had had to move on and on for new jobs, until finally it became easier just to move, to move for the moving. Perhaps this world has gone now; one never hears of it. Perhaps wartime prosperity has wiped it out; I do not know. In the 'thirties it was a vast, submerged, secondary United States with its own categories of cities, advertised by its own kind of chambers of commerce, its own recognized leaders, its strong men and its recognized bad men, its ragged dowagers and grimy debutantes, and its own laws—such as they were—which dealt primarily with self-preservation. The true world of private enterprise and individual initiative. It will come back, unless America is very wise, but next time it may have lost its "picturesque" quality; they may not beg cap in hand; they may fight with something else but razors because they will know other weapons, and they may not confine their fighting to themselves.

The King of Tramps

There were strange men among them, remarkable men, unknown to the rest of America. No one has written the biography of Tex, King of Tramps, for example. I never saw him, but I knew there was an obsession in him not unlike Hitler's, a terrible straining of the ego to find expression—either that or he was a wandering imbecile having a glorious time. At least fifty times in the course of a couple of thousand miles I came across his insigne, his coat of arms: Tex—KT. You would find it carved on the wooden seat of a privy on the edge of a Nevada town, penciled on the wall of a shower room in a Salvation Army flophouse in Idaho, chalked on the iron side of a locomotive tender in South Dakota, painted in six-foot letters of red on a white cliffside high up in a Montana canyon. Men told me you found it from Maine to California, everywhere, printed, written, carved thousands of times in the course of what must have been fifteen or twenty years of wandering.

In the jungle, cities were judged and rated on the basis of

their citizens' generosity with handouts and the temperament of the railway "deeks"[dicks—police] who guard the freight yards. You did not, for example, attempt to travel through Cheyenne, Wyoming, if you had any alternative. You were apt to be chased from the yards there not only with clubs, which was fairly common, but with revolver shots, and it was a long walk to the next station. You traveled through a certain Idaho town only at careful intervals to avoid the monthly raid by the sheriff, who filled his jail with indigents, fed them on nineteen cents a day, and collected a dollar a day from the local government for each occupant. There was no rancor against the sheriff—he had to have his dodge, his racket, like everybody else—but you just avoided him, unless, of course, the weather was rugged and handouts were not forthcoming and you desired a month indoors with steady meals.

Hobo Lore

One of the most renowned and fearsome characters to dwellers in the jungle was Humpy Davis, railway dick at Harvey, North Dakota. He, it appeared, was a bearlike hunchback, who took a fiendish pride in his ability to clean out a crowded box car, single-handed, in one minute flat. Normally he used a club, and the score of broken arms and heads was running extremely high, when a conclave of hoboes out in Vancouver decided that Humpy must be eliminated for the good of all concerned. They elected a tall Negro, famous for his marksmanship, to do the job. News travels fast by the jungle grapevine. Humpy knew, and waited. One day he observed a Negro, alone, walking steadily toward him between the tracks. This was it. Humpy stood still, letting him come on. Suddenly the Negro stopped, swung up his hand, and fired. The legend relates that Humpy did not move, did not raise his arm. Instead, he shouted: "Shoot at my head, you black bastard, shoot at my head!" The assassin fired again. Humpy, unmoving, repeated his instruction. The Negro fired his six shots, yelled in astonishment and terror and, as he began to run, was brought down by a single shot. Humpy walked across the yards to a beer parlor, unbuttoned his shirt, and exhibited his bulletproof vest with six indentations over the heart so closely grouped that a coffee mug could cover them all. It is a favorite story in the jungle. If one doubts it, he is wise not to express his doubt.

My empty box car at Sparks rapidly filled, the train operators having deliberately left it open and vacant in order to avoid having the inevitable load of hoboes clambering around on top of the cars or clinging to the tender. All were bums by choice save one weather-beaten couple of advanced age who came from New Mexico. They had just lost their small farm and were looking for new opportunities. The man carried a great pack with a washboard strapped on it, while his wizened little wife held their scabby hound dog by a length of frayed clothesline. They represented Respectability among us, were accorded a whole corner to themselves and not included in the unending argument, jeering, boasting, and scuffling.

Services Rendered

I sat in the open doorway, swinging my legs in the sun, and listened to a youngster of sixteen. He was well built, with a remarkably attractive, open face, which had a way of slipping quickly into a sneer, becoming then almost sinister. He was boasting of his racket, and I was failing to understand. Finally he took out a crumpled sheet of paper. I read: "For services rendered, I have delivered the following articles to—[the boy]." Then came a list including watch, fountain pen, set of evening clothes, silver-backed hairbrushes, and so on. "That was in Frisco last month," the boy explained. "I work fast. I find the café where the queers go, mix in with the bunch that looks richest, go home with one of them, and before I get through with him he's given me everything he owns and the written statement. I'm a minor. It's a criminal offense. But he can't do a thing about it, not a thing." He discussed it openly, casually, as if he were boasting of his prowess at baseball. I had only the vaguest notion of what homosexuality was all about, had never been acquainted with anyone I knew to be abnormal in this way, and rather imagined it was something confined to certain boys' schools in England and the bohemian quarters of Paris. Suddenly it was all around me. I noticed men with glazed, slightly bulging eyes and uncertain voices who traveled in company with boys in their teens. The men were referred to as "wolves" (long before that word became slang for Casanovas of normal physiology). A Negro boy named Freddie, no more than fourteen, joined our group one day. He was complaining loudly about the perfidy of a white man who had picked him up while he had been hitchhiking the evening before. "Offered me a quarter if he could—, then he wouldn't give me the quarter, the skunk. Kicked me out of his car. But I slammed a rock through his back window, the bastard," Freddie finished boastfully, and was rewarded by general acknowledgment that it had served the so-and-so right. All this told so naturally, as if it were an open, common matter understood and accepted by everyone. Except for me, apparently it was.

Freddie was very nearly the cause of my death one night. We had reassembled in the box car after a brief foray through a bleak Nevada hamlet, and now, as the train rumbled through the night, we squatted around a small fire in the middle of the car floor, exchanging tidbits. Freddie was missing; somebody thought he had caught the train at the other end, and when we heard a banging on the roof we knew he had, and that he had run over the tops, leaping in the darkness from car to car. Somebody slid the big door wide open, and we heard Freddie yell: "Grab my legs, I'm coming down." We looked at one another. There was silence for a moment. A man said: "How about you, Slim? You got long arms." I had no choice of action. I stood by the door, while a chain of three or four men fastened themselves to one of my legs. The wind blew in my face. The train was racketing along a narrow bridge over a dark canyon. Suddenly there were Freddie's dangling feet, then his legs, swinging in close, then away again as the box car tilted, then close again. I grabbed them, felt myself being torn out of the car, then was toppled over backwards, on top of the human chain, Freddie on top of me. Except for a moment, ten years later, when I found myself at the door of a plunging airplane, trying to jump, I have never known a greater terror. Freddie had stolen a bottle of cherry brandy. He was the hero of the evening, and we ate, drank, and sang to the accompaniment of a harmonica until long after midnight.

Catching the Hot Shot

I was traveling with two boys of seventeen, bound like myself for Minneapolis where they had recently been suspended from high school for unauthorized absences. We had made a secret pact: they did the begging for food (at which they were expert) and, whenever there was no time to beg or the fruits were meager, I would buy food for the three of us from my store of six or eight dollars which was tied in a handkerchief and secured out of sight inside my belt. (Murder for much less than that was a commonplace in the jungle.) One night we sat by the rails of the "Oregon Short Line," next to the water tank on the outskirts of Ogden, Utah, where we knew our train would pause. We were after the manifest, the "hot shot"—a sealed, nonstop freight train, representing to this social dimension what the Century does to another. We became aware that an enormous Negro was standing a few feet away. He said: "Good evening," sat down beside us, and chewed on a straw. Eventually he said: "Catching the hot shot?" I said we were. Finally: "Rode it once myself. Long, cold ride. Get mighty hungry." More silence and then he said casually: "Tell you what. One you boys want to walk over to my house, have my wife fix up a few sandwiches for you." I got up and said that was kind of him and that I would go along. My companions said nothing.

We walked along a narrow road, bordered by weeds and ditches. He seemed to be in no hurry and said nothing. I was worried about missing the train and asked him where his house was. "See that light?" he answered. The light appeared to be at least a half-mile away. We walked on, and it began to seem very strange to me. Why should a Negro, obviously poor, go so much out of his way to aid three young white tramps? I was becoming very uneasy, trying to think of some way to withdraw, when the man turned abruptly, walked across a plank over the ditch, and halted by a clump of willows. "Come here a minute, Slim," he said.

My throat had become suddenly dry and I could not answer. He called in a soft tone two or three times: "Come here—got something to show you." All manner of ideas flashed through my head. Did he know about my money and intend to murder me for it? Had he some grisly object there he wanted me to carry away on the train?

He walked deliberately back and stood towering over me so close I could smell his breath. "Want to make a quarter, Slim?" he said softly, coaxingly.

My voice returned enough for me to say in what I hoped were even tones that I couldn't do anything for him. I turned and began to walk back down the dark roadway, the hair on the back of my neck tickling, expecting something to strike me at any moment. Then two figures stepped from the ditch and stood there, waiting, in my path. My heart beat faster, but my head got very cool. I had walked into a trap and was about to be "rolled." I kept on, approached them, lifted my hands over my head, and said in an abnormally confident voice: "All right. You can have anything I have on me."

One of them said: "For Christ sakes, Slim, what do you think you're doing?"

My two loyal, very wise companions had followed us. They got out their knives and wanted to attack the Negro, but let themselves be dissuaded. They scolded me at length for being so dumb that I hadn't recognized a queer, and I had nothing to say. My hands shook for an hour afterwards.

Good Times and Bad

There were glorious days of sunshine, days when we stretched out nude on a flat car cooled by chunks of ice someone tossed down from the "reefer"[refrigerator car] adjoining, days when we swung our legs idly and yelled to the girls working in the passing fields, days when we abandoned the trains and swam naked in deep mountain pools of cold, clear water. In the night there was hazard and danger, always. There was a midnight halt while the train reorganized at a sleeping Montana division point on the Milwaukee line. The hoboes gathered in a hamburger shop, the only concern still open for business. It was a cold night. With their pennies and nickels the tramps provided themselves with thick mugs of coffee. I ordered sandwiches for myself and my companions. Then to my horror I discovered I had only a five-dollar bill. I passed it over the fake marble counter to the waiter as surreptitiously as I could, and no one noticed. But Montana is a silver state, and the waiter returned with four heavy, gleaming silver dollars in his hand. He did not put them in my anxiously outthrust palm but proceeded to drop them, ringing, clattering on the counter, one at a time. I was conscious that the sounds of eating and drinking around me had ceased and that every eye had turned in my direction. I stuffed them in my pocket and we rose, leaving our food unfinished, sauntered out the door and then ran with all our strength to the train. We hurried along from car to car, scrambling, panting, until we found one with the door unlocked. It was half-filled with lumber. We climbed in, shifted the boards until we had made a hole, then pulled them over us. As the train began its slow, jerking start we heard boots scuffling the boards above our heads. Later we could catch a few words. The voices we recognized as belonging to two of the more evil-looking tramps of the earlier evening. They were talking about the kids with the silver dollars. The voices ceased after a time, and we drifted to uneasy, uncomfortable sleep. In the morning the men were gone.

I arrived at my father's house with my face black from the coal dust of a locomotive tender—my berth during the final roaring, kaleidoscopic night of clinging to a passenger express. Those were my last deliberately sought adventures, but they were not my last adventures. In distant countries I had never seen, the whirlpool of our times was beginning to move in the increasingly rapid, spreading gyration which was to engulf my whole generation and throw its members upon a thousand reefs. I had seen heartbreak, violence, and death in their individual forms, but the dictionary had not yet included as a generic term the word Fascism.

Chapter 6

The New Deal

Chapter Preface

When Franklin Delano Roosevelt was elected to office in 1932, the entire country seemed to breathe a sigh of relief. Finally, here was somebody who was proposing to do something about the Depression, as opposed to wishing it away with pointless predictions. Roosevelt even used the radio to ease panic and tell the American public what he and his advisers were doing about the problems that plagued the country. Roosevelt's "Fireside Chats" were given extra weight by the fact that they were followed by action and observable results. This could be attributed to the fact that everybody was cooperating with the New Dealers. Congress, who had been taking flak from the public for inaction for so long, now gave Roosevelt a blank check to "just do anything," as he had once asked for in one of his campaign speeches. Even the press was cooperating. Roosevelt had contracted poliomyelitis, a viral infection of the spinal cord, and could not walk without the help of leg braces. The press agreed to keep Roosevelt's physical disability out of the papers, noting that it was important that nothing diminish the public's faith in the president during the crisis.

Roosevelt brought a team of advisers with him to the White House. Most of them were professors from Columbia who got placed in various posts in Washington. The press labeled them the "Brain Trust" and together they assembled the New Deal out of various social and economic theories. None of the New Dealers knew for certain if the programs they created would work. It was a completely new and more active role for government than had ever been tried before. Although many of the New Deal programs were struck down as unconstitutional by the Supreme Court, they paved the way for many of the social programs alive today.

Bold, Persistent Experimentation

Rexford G. Tugwell

When Roosevelt became president he brought with him an elite group of advisors which the press nicknamed the Brain Trust. The main members were Raymond Moley, Adolph A. Berle Jr., and Rexford G. Tugwell. They were all professors from Columbia University. Roosevelt and his Brain Trust formulated experimental political and economic solutions to the nation's problems. These policies and programs became the New Deal. Tugwell had been brought on as secretary of agriculture and was key in forging new farm policies as well as contributing to the other New Deal programs. The following excerpt is from Tugwell's book about the administration's first year in office.

The depression had been going on since 1929, but its most frightening happenings were now reaching something of a climax. The strange, lost feeling nearly everyone had was becoming chronic; actually, distress was just reaching the centers of the economy. It was no longer something merely reported to financiers and upper executives; it had invaded their own safe enclaves.

Since the worth of capital was determined by what was produced, property values fell when production stopped. There seemed to be no bottom to the market for the stocks and bonds that represented businesses. Since holdings could not be disposed of except at a sacrifice, most of their obligations could not be met. This was repeated over and over in business circles (with overtones of despair) that "values must be restored." All this could possibly mean, however, was that securities must be given higher value by the earnings of the enterprises they represented. This was, of course, the theme I kept repeating, that earnings would only resume when there were customers for goods and services. The millions of unemployed and their families were not buyers. It was a tight round of logic; I insisted that it could only be broken into by the one agency with the power to create and distribute income—the federal government.

Gradually I became discouraged because I could see that Roosevelt was trying to find another way out of the dilemma, and I knew what it was. Adolf detailed it for him, and it was, of course, something I could see well enough as being possible. This was an induced rise in prices to liquidate the heavy burden of debt, unfreeze assets, and thus allow a new start. We differed in that I thought the best way to do this was by creating employment. This did mean temporarily unbalanced budgets, but there was nothing sacred about an annual budget that I could see. If a balance was reached within a few years, that was satisfactory.

In this argument I used a simile I had found effective in a recent address at Teachers College of Columbia University. I had said that Hoover's activities (I had in mind mostly the Reconstruction Finance Corporation) were like putting fertilizer up in the branches of a tree. Government loans to financial institutions and industrial concerns were treetop operations; what was needed was to feed the roots. The workers, including the unemployed, were the ones to be cared for. And, Adolf added, the small enterprisers, who felt the worst of the squeeze because they were closest to the consumer who could not buy.

A Bottom Up Approach

I believed there had to be unemployment relief on an enormous scale. Also the government would need to be what amounted to a residual employer, giving jobs as well as cash for living expenses. It could only be done federally, partly because states would not tackle it in a uniform way, but mostly because they had used up their funds, just as New York had. If loans were made to businesses, most of the yield would go to the liquidation of debts; after that the resumption of activity would depend on the initiative of enterprisers. This, I contended, was an indirect, slow, and uncertain process.

This led to an argument about financing. It was agreed that in the long run—I admitted that it might be quite a long run—tax yields from increased productivity would more than pay for the relief expenditures, but there was no escaping the first, the beginning cost. There was another objection I had to meet. If the government printed money and distributed it as relief or in payment for public works, that would result in inflation, which meant higher prices and discouraged consumers. This was a true dilemma, and one for which I had no very satisfactory answer. I simply said that workers would rather pay higher prices than have no incomes at all. It could be explained to them that the one was the condition of having the other. I could see that a political candidate wouldn't like to make such a complex explanation, but there was this: he could promise incomes at once, and the inflation would be delayed. If productivity increased fast enough, the rise of prices might not be so important.

Besides, I argued, there could be a revision of taxes, with higher rates for large incomes. The yield, of course, could not possibly be enough to pay for the needed relief. There was no escaping the conclusion that if anything really remedial was to be done, it must start with a massive enlargement of buying power furnished by federal funds, and with immediate price rises. This would have to be endured; it was another kind of taxation. Such a program might have the same eventual result as the devaluation of the dollar being advocated by [Yale economist] Irving Fisher, who wanted a commodity dollar instead of a gold one, or the Cornellians [economic theorists from Cornell University], who (mistakenly, I thought) believed that the dollar could be given higher value by the manipulation of its gold content.

There was no reason why institutions guarding people's savings could not be protected by moratoria, or why mortgage foreclosures could not be checked until production was resumed. Easier bankruptcy proceedings would allow small enterprises to write off old debts and make a new start. Still, everything depended on that initial injection of purchasing power, and it had to be a massive one.

Where to Get the Money?

Roosevelt annoyed us—or at least Ray and myself, not Adolf so much—by persistently coming back to monetary devices taken by themselves. We were at heart believers in sound money. Greenbackism was part of the populist tradition that we hoped had been left behind. We knew well enough that it hadn't; its advocates were loud and growing louder; all the old schemes for cheapening money were apparently still alive, and there were many new ones. The Governor [Roosevelt; he had been governor of New York] wanted to know about all of them. We shuddered and got him the information.

Actually, I had long since been converted to Fisher's commodity dollar—that is, one having the general backing of many other commodities besides gold. This would give it a more stable value from one time to another, since the value of gold fluctuated wildly. But a time of crisis such as the present was not the time to make such a drastic change.

Roosevelt had us in a difficult spot when we argued for increased purchasing power and at the same time opposed what we chose to call greenbacks. Where was the government to get the dollars it paid out for public employment or relief? Either it must have increased income or it must simply print the currency it distributed. It was all very well to argue that increased productivity would in time yield the income. But that would not be until the funds had been provided that would eventually increase the national product. Temporarily, we were advocating an issue of greenbacks—weren't we?

Of course we were. When I spoke of higher income taxes, especially on the large incomes, I knew how small the increased revenue would be. No, there was no way out of it. There must simply be a distribution of printed money. But, we insisted, it would be temporary.

We were not monetary theorists, and we said so repeatedly. Ray did round up and escort to Albany some of those whose field it was; they were not brought so often during the spring as later when we got down to the issues judged best to be met in speeches; still, we could not really avoid the issue. It became more acute after Irving Fisher, who now had begun to talk about "reflation," made his way uninvited to Albany and spent some time with Roosevelt. Fisher had become something of a fanatic, and Roosevelt always enjoyed talking to fanatics. The impression this visit made was one we knew would have consequences. In fact, we had to deal with it at once, since Roosevelt would not let it alone.

Price Fixing in the Public Interest

It was more and more obvious, he insisted, that a total effort of some sort to lift values would have to be undertaken. There was no other way to liquefy assets, to get rid of debts, and generally to activate enterprise. I came back to asking whether he did not realize that this meant raised prices for potential consumers before they had been made actual consumers by having incomes to spend. My fear was that dependence on a program of this sort could postpone any extensive effort to provide public works or relief benefits. Recovery would at least be delayed, and this could no longer be afforded. As long as relief was regarded as a philanthrophy—a dole, as the Republicans preferred to call it—it would never be the boost needed for recovery.

Roosevelt was inclined to argue that raising prices would draw wages up to their new levels, and that the same rule would hold about relief: there would be an irresistible demand for increases. I objected that any such wage increases would be gained only by costly strikes and industrial disturbances As for relief, the unemployed had no leverage. Besides, I reminded him, any gross general changes would have different results in particular industries that could not be foreseen. This was economists' language for saying that prices would respond to pressure in different degrees. Some would not respond at all; others would be too responsive. But the resulting situation might be no better than it was now. Exchange among economic groups would be constantly disrupted. Those with more advantages would tend to stifle those with fewer or none.

This brought us, on several occasions, to further discussions of planning for fair and stable exchange, a topic much on the minds of some thoughtful industrialists and bankers—among them Gerard Swope of General Electric, Henry I. Harriman, president of the United States Chamber of Commerce, and Fred I. Kent, the banker. There was, in fact, such an array of respectable support that the possibilities could be discussed with some feeling of approval in high places. The detractors of that sort of planning called it price-fixing, and they had a point; but it was price-fixing in the public interest. At the same time it was thoroughly inconsistent with orthodox progressivism, which held that fixing prices should be forbidden as conspiratorial. Prices were supposed to be fixed in the competition among sellers and buyers. If the planning was approached by way of Swope's ideas or, as I reminded Roosevelt, those he himself had put forward when he was arguing for a Construction Council, it was a serious departure from the principles of [Associate Justice of the Supreme Court Louis] Brandeis and his supporters [who followed Woodrow Wilson's New Freedom economic doctrine which tried to restore competition in an economy plagued by monopolies]. They could be expected to object and to rally the old Wilsonian forces.

Roosevelt was at least willing to talk about an integrated system even if it did involve accepting a holistic conception of the economy. Its devices would be a complete reversal of antitrust policies. I had no desire to apologize for this, since the gain I could point to would be that we should have an organism rather than chaos. In such a scheme, progress based on increases in productivity might be encouraged, and the ups and downs of the business cycle might be smoothed out. The scheme had attractions, and I enlarged on them whenever I got the chance. Roosevelt joined in the argument readily. It was evident, however, that he would make up his mind about the feasibility of an integrated system after considering many other views than ours.

"Brandeis again!" Ray said when we talked about the political implications.

The First Year: 1933

Eleanor Roosevelt

Franklin Delano Roosevelt had been stricken with polio in 1921 and was nearly paralyzed. He could not walk without the help of braces—a Depression-era secret that the press honored for the good of the country. Eleanor Roosevelt became the eyes and ears of her husband during his three terms as president. She traveled around the country talking to people and reporting on social and economic conditions. The experience prompted Eleanor to take a more active role in helping people. In fact, she soon became so active in promoting humanitarian causes that her own reputation rivaled that of her husband. The following excerpt is taken from her autobiography and describes the Roosevelt's first frantic year in office. She discusses the effect her husband's programs had on the country and her visits with the returning Bonus March veterans.

During the early White House days when I was busy with organizing my side of the household, my husband was meeting one problem after another. It had a most exhilarating effect on him. Decisions were being made, new ideas were being tried, people were going to work and businessmen who ordinarily would have scorned government assistance were begging the government to find solutions for their problems.

What was interesting to me about the administration of those days was the willingness of everyone to co-operate with everyone else. As conditions grew better, of course, people's attitudes changed, but fundamentally it was that spirit of co-operation that pulled us out of the depression. Congress, which traditionally never has a long honeymoon with a new president, even when the political majority is of his party, went along during those first few months, delegating powers to the President and passing legislation that it would never have passed except during a crisis.

The Good Neighbor

Soon after the inauguration of 1933 we began to have a succession of visitors whom after dinner Franklin would take upstairs to his study. There were two reasons why these particular people were invited to the White House those first years. One was that the economic and political situation in the world made it necessary for him to establish contacts with the leaders of other countries; the other was his desire to build new contacts for better understanding on this continent and abroad.

For the heads of nations, Franklin worked out a reception which he thought made them feel that the United States recognized the importance of their governments. If the guests arrived in the afternoon we had tea for the entire party; afterwards, all but the most important guests went to a hotel or to their own embassy. Later Blair House, across Pennsylvania Avenue, was acquired by the government and arranged for the use of important visitors. The head of a government spent one night in the White House, accompanied by his wife if she was with him. There usually was a state dinner with conversation or music afterwards. The following morning Franklin and his guest would often have another talk before the guest went over to Blair House or to his embassy.

One of our first guests in 1933 was [British prime minister] Ramsay MacDonald, who came with his daughter, Ishbel. We enjoyed meeting him, but even then we sensed in him a certain weariness. The loss of his wife had been a great blow to him. In many ways his daughter was a more vivid and vital person than he.

I think Franklin believed even then that it was most important for the English-speaking nations of the world to understand one another, whether the crisis was economic or, as later, military. This did not mean that he always agreed with the policies of these other countries; but he recognized the importance to us and to them of good feeling and understanding and co-operation.

The prime minister of Canada also came to stay with us that first spring, so that he and my husband and the prime minister of Great Britain could more or less co-ordinate their common interests.

In the same period Edouard Herriot, the French statesman, also arrived in Washington. As I look over the lists of what seem to be an unbelievable number of guests that first year, I find that we received an Italian mission, a German mission, and a Chinese mission, and even a Japanese envoy who came to lunch. Other guests included the governor general of the Philippines, Frank Murphy, later on the Supreme Court, who brought with him Manuel Quezon; the prime minister of New Zealand, who came with his wife to lunch; and His Highness Prince Ras Desta Dember, special ambassador of the Emperor of Ethiopia.

The President of Panama also paid us a visit. He was not the only guest from our own hemisphere. There was a stag dinner for the Brazilian delegation; we received a special ambassador from the Argentine; the Mexican envoy came to lunch; and the Brazilian envoy returned, after a trip through the country, to report on his travels.

Franklin had a deep conviction that we must learn to understand and to get on with our neighbors in this hemisphere. He believed it was up to us, who had been to blame in many ways for a big brother attitude which was not acceptable to our neighbors, to make the first effort. So even at that early date he was beginning to lay down through personal contacts the policy of the Good Neighbor, which was to become of increasing importance.

From the time we moved to Washington in 1933, [Chief of Staff] Louis Howe became more and more of an invalid. At first he was able to be in his office and to keep his finger on much that was going on, and the second bonus march on Washington by the veterans of World War I he handled personally.

The first march, which had taken place in Mr. Hoover's administration, was still fresh in everybody's mind. I shall never forget my feeling of horror when I learned that the Army had actually been ordered to evict the veterans from their encampment. In the chaos that followed, the veterans' camp on the Anacostia flats was burned and many people were injured, some of them seriously. This one incident shows what fear can make people do, for Mr. Hoover was a Quaker, who abhorred violence, and General MacArthur, his chief of staff, must have known how many veterans would resent the order and never forget it. They must have known, too, the effect it would have on public opinion.

When the second bonus march took place in March of 1933 I was greatly worried for fear nothing would be done to prevent a similar tragedy. However, after talking the situation over with Louis Howe, Franklin immediately decided that the veterans should be housed in an old camp and provided with food through the relief administration. Louis spent hours talking with the leaders. I think they held their meetings in a government auditorium and were heard by the proper people in Congress. As a result, everything was orderly.

Although Louis often asked me to take him for a drive in the afternoon, I was rather surprised one day when he insisted that I drive him out to the veterans' camp just off Potomac Drive. When we arrived he announced that he was going to sit in the car but that I was to walk around among the veterans and see just how things were. Hesitatingly I got out and walked over to where I saw a line-up of men waiting for food. They looked at me curiously and one of them asked my name and what I wanted. When I said I just wanted to see how they were getting on, they asked me to join them.

After their bowls were filled with food, I followed them into the big eating hall. I was invited to say a few words to them—I think I mentioned having gone over the battle fronts in 1919—and then they sang for me some of the old army songs. After lunch I was asked to look into several other buildings, and finally we came to the hospital that had been set up for them.

I did not spend as much as an hour there; then I got into the car and drove away. Everyone waved and I called, "Good luck," and they answered, "Good-by and good luck to you." There had been no excitement, and my only protection had been a weary gentleman, Louis Howe, who had slept in the car during my entire visit.

Eleanor Roosevelt's tireless efforts on behalf of President Roosevelt were not only a benefit to him, but to the entire nation as well.

Most of us who watched Louis could tell that he was failing. He sat a good deal of the time in his room, surrounded by newspapers, but up to the last few months his advice was still valuable. He died on April 18, 1936, at the naval hospital in Washington. He had lived in the White House until a short time before his death.

I always felt that the loss of Louis's influence and knowledge and companionship was a great blow to my husband.

Louis had seemed to have an acute sense of the need for keeping a balance in Franklin's appointments, making sure that my husband saw a cross section of people and heard a variety of points of view. While Louis was alive, I had fewer complaints from various groups that they had been excluded than ever again. Considering how many people want to see the President and how hard it is to keep some semblance of balance, I think Louis did a remarkable job. He tried to see that all points of view reached Franklin so that he would make no decision without full consideration.

It Wasn't Always Safe

The President's wife does not go out informally except on rare occasions to old friends. Now and then, in the spring, Elinor Morgenthau and I stole away in my car or hers, and stopped in at some little place for lunch or tea. Driving my own car was one of the issues the Secret Service people and I had a battle about at the very start. The Secret Service prefers to have an agent go with the President's wife, but I did not want either a chauffeur or a Secret Service agent always with me; I never did consent to having a Secret Service agent.

After the head of the Secret Service found I was not going to allow an agent to accompany me everywhere, he went one day to Louis Howe, plunked a revolver down on the table and said, "Well, all right, if Mrs. Roosevelt is going to drive around the country alone, at least ask her to carry this in the car." I carried it religiously and during the summer I asked a friend, a man who had been one of Franklin's bodyguards in New York State, to give me some practice in target shooting so that if the need arose I would know how to use the gun. After considerable practice, I finally learned to hit a target. I would never have used it on a human being, but I thought I ought to know how to handle a revolver if I had to have one in my possession.

Always, when my husband and I met after a trip that either of us had taken, we tried to arrange for an uninterrupted meal so that we could hear the whole story while it was fresh and not dulled by repetition. That I became, as the years went by, a better reporter and a better observer was largely owing to the fact that Franklin's questions covered such a wide range. I found myself obliged to notice everything. For instance, when I returned from a trip around the Gaspé [an area in Quebec, Canada], he wanted to know not only what kind of fishing and hunting was possible in that area but what the life of the fisherman was, what he had to eat, how he lived, what the farms were like, how the houses were built, what type of education was available, and whether it was completely church-controlled like the rest of the life in the village.

When I spoke of Maine, he wanted to know about everything I had seen on the farms I visited, the kinds of homes and the types of people, how the Indians seemed to be getting on and where they came from.

Franklin never told me I was a good reporter nor, in the early days, were any of my trips made at his request. I realized, however, that he would not question me so closely if he were not interested, and I decided this was the only way I could help him, outside of running the house, which was soon organized and running itself under Mrs. Nesbitt.

Evidence of Relief

In the autumn I was invited by the Quakers to investigate the conditions that they were making an effort to remedy in the coal-mining areas of West Virginia. My husband agreed that it would be a good thing to do, so the visit was arranged. I had not been photographed often enough then to be recognized, so I was able to spend a whole day going about the area near Morgantown, West Virginia, without anyone's discovering who I was.

The conditions I saw convinced me that with a little leadership there could develop in the mining areas, if not a people's revolution, at least a people's party patterned after some of the previous parties born of bad economic conditions. There were men in that area who had been on relief for from three to five years and who had almost forgotten what it was like to have a job at which they could work for more than one or two days a week. There were children who did not know what it was to sit down at a table and eat a proper meal.

Visiting a Mining Village

One story which I brought home from that trip I recounted at the dinner table one night. In a company house I visited, where the people had evidently seen better days, the man showed me his weekly pay slips. A small amount had been deducted toward his bill at the company store and for his rent and for oil for his mine lamp. These deductions left him less than a dollar in cash each week. There were six children in the family, and they acted as though they were afraid of strangers. I noticed a bowl on the table filled with scraps, the kind that you or I might give to a dog, and I saw children, evidently looking for their noonday meal, take a handful out of that bowl and go out munching. That was all they had to eat.

As I went out, two of the children had gathered enough courage to stand by the door, the little boy holding a white rabbit in his arms. It was evident that it was a most cherished pet. The little girl was thin and scrawny, and had a gleam in her eyes as she looked at her brother. She said, "He thinks we are not going to eat it, but we are," and at that the small boy fled down the road clutching the rabbit closer than ever.

It happened that [diplomat] William C. Bullitt was at dinner that night and I have always been grateful to him for the check he sent me the next day, saying he hoped it might help to keep the rabbit alive.

This trip to the mining areas was my first contact with the work being done by the Quakers. I liked the theory of trying to put people to work to help themselves. The men were started on projects and taught to use their abilities to develop new skills. The women were encouraged to revive any household arts they might once have known but which they had neglected in the drab life of the mining village.

This was only the first of many trips into the mining districts but it was the one that started the homestead idea. The University of West Virginia, in Morgantown, had already created a committee to help the miners on the Quaker agricultural project. With that committee and its experience as a nucleus, the government obtained the loan of one of the university's people, Mr. Bushrod Grimes, and established the Resettlement Administration. Louis Howe created a small advisory committee on which I, Mr. Pickett, and others served. It was all experimental work, but it was designed to get people off relief, to put them to work building their own homes and to give them enough land to start growing food.

It was hoped that business would help by starting on each of these projects an industry in which some of the people could find regular work. A few small industries were started but they were not often successful. Only a few of the resettlement projects had any measure of success; nevertheless, I have always felt that the good they did was incalculable. Conditions were so nearly the kind that breed revolution that the men and women needed to be made to feel their government's interest and concern.

I began to hear very serious reports of conditions in Logan County, West Virginia, where for many years whole families had been living in tents because they had been evicted from company houses after a strike. All the men had been blacklisted and could not get work anywhere; they were existing on the meager allowance that the State of West Virginia provided for the unemployed. Now the tents were worn out, illness was rampant, and no one had any medical care. Finally Mrs. Leonard Elmhirst [a philanthropist who was involved in many radical causes] and I established a clinic to take care of the children. When I told my husband of the conditions there he said to talk to [New Deal administrator] Harry Hopkins and to tell him that these families must be out of tents by Christmas. It was done, and for two years, out of my radio money and Mrs. Elmhirst's generosity, we tried to remedy among the children the effects of conditions which had existed for many years.

I came to know very well a stream near Morgantown

called Scott's Run, or Bloody Run, because of the violent strikes that once occurred in the mines there. Some of the company houses perched on hills on either side of the run, seemed scarcely fit for human habitation. The homestead project started near Morgantown was called Arthurdale and took in people from all the nearby mining villages.

One of the first people to go to Arthurdale was [Presidential advisor] Bernard M. Baruch, who helped me to establish the original school and always took a great interest in the project, even visiting it without me on some occasions. I have always hoped that he got as much satisfaction as I did out of the change in the children after they had been living on the project for six months.

The homestead projects were attacked in Congress, for

Please Give This Your Immediate Attention

At the peak of the Depression a quarter of the workforce was out of work. Millions of desperate Americans who could not pay their bills or even feed themselves wrote letters to President Roosevelt begging for assistance. The following letter was written by a woman in Picayune, Mississippi. It was taken from Andrew Carroll's anthology, Letters of a Nation.

Honorable Franklin D. Roosevelt.
Washington, D.C.
Dear Mr. President:

I am forced to write to you because we find ourselves in *a very serious condition*. For the last three or four years we have had depression and *suffered* with my *family* and little children *severely*. Now Since the Home Owners Loan Corporation [New Deal organization created to protect home owners from foreclosure] opened up, I have been going there in order to save my home, because there has been unemployment in my house for more than three years. You can imagine that I and my family have suffered from lack of water supply in my house for more than two years. Last winter the most part by men who had never seen for themselves the plight of the miners or what we were trying to do for them. There is no question that much money was spent, perhaps some of it unwisely. The projects were all experimental. In Arthurdale, for instance, though the University of West Virginia recommended the site, apparently nobody knew what was afterwards discovered—that there was a substratum of porous rock which finally caused great expense in making the water supply safe. Nevertheless, I have always felt that many human beings who might have cost us thousands of dollars in tuberculosis sanitariums, insane asylums, and jails were restored to usefulness and given confidence in themselves. Later, when during World War II, I met boys from that area I could not help thinking that

---

I did not have coal and the pipes burst in my house and therefore could not make heat in the house. Now winter is here again and we are suffering of cold, no water in the house, and we are facing to be forced out of the house, because I have no money to move or pay so much money as they want when after making settlement I am mother of little children, am sick and losing my health, and we are eight people in the family, and where can I go when I don't have money because no one is working in my house. The Home Loan Corporation wants $42. a month rent or else we will have to be on the street. I am living in this house for about ten years and when times were good we would put our last cent in the house and now I have *no money, no home and no wheres to go.* I beg of you to please help me and my family and little children for the sake of a sick mother and suffering family to give this your immediate attention so we will not be forced to move or put out in the street.

Waiting and Hoping that you will act quickly.

Thanking you very much I remain

Mrs. E. L.

Andrew Carroll, ed., *Letters of a Nation: A Collection of Extraordinary American Letters.* New York: Kodansha America, 1997.

a great many of them were able to serve their country only because of the things that had been done to help their parents through the depression period.

Nothing we learn in this world is ever wasted and I have come to the conclusion that practically nothing we do ever stands by itself. If it is good, it will serve some good purpose in the future. If it is evil, it may haunt us and handicap our efforts in unimagined ways.

Years later, after the Social Security Act was passed, I saw how it worked in individual cases in this area. There was a mine accident in which several men were killed, and my husband asked me to go down and find out what the people were saying. One man received the Carnegie medal posthumously because he had gone back into the mine to help rescue other men. His widow had several children, so her social security benefits would make her comfortable. In talking to another widow who had three children and a fourth about to be born, I asked how she was going to manage. She seemed quite confident and told me: "My sister and her two children will come to live with us. I am going to get social security benefits of nearly sixty-five dollars a month. I pay fifteen dollars a month on my house and land, and I shall raise vegetables and have chickens and with the money from the government I will get along very well. In the past probably the mine company might have given me a small check and often the other miners took up a collection if they could afford it, but this income from the government I can count on until my children are grown."

Two other events of that first autumn in Washington stand out in my mind. On November 17, 1933, Henry Morgenthau, Jr., was sworn in as undersecretary of the treasury in the Oval Room in the White House, thus starting on his long and arduous labors in the Treasury Department. When Secretary Woodin resigned, Henry Morgenthau succeeded him and held the office until shortly after my husband's death, when he also resigned and left Washington.

On that same day my husband and [Soviet diplomat] Mr. Litvinov held the final conversations on the recognition of the Soviet Union. There was considerable excitement over the first telephone conversation between the two countries which took place between Mr. Litvinov in the White House and his wife and son in Russia. The ushers noted it in their daily record book because, while there had been overseas conversations with many other European countries, this was the opening of diplomatic relations with Russia.

Needless to say, among some of my husband's old friends there was considerable opposition to the recognition of Russia. His mother came to him before the announcement was made to tell him she had heard rumors that he was about to recognize Russia, but that she felt this would be a disastrous move and widely misunderstood by the great majority of their old friends.

Not only his old friends but with various other people my husband had frequent run-ins over the new theory that government had a responsibility to the people. I remember that when Senator Carter Glass insisted that Virginia needed no relief, Franklin suggested that he take a drive with him to see some of the bad spots. The senator never accepted his invitation.

The opening of diplomatic relations with Russia and our relations in this hemisphere were the administration's first points of attack in our foreign policy, but the major emphasis in those early years was and had to be on questions of domestic policy and our internal economic recovery.

The Most Successful Agency

As I look back over the actual measures undertaken in this first year I realize that the one in which my husband took the greatest pleasure was the establishment on April 5, 1933, of the Civilian Conservation Corps camps. The teen-age youngster, the boy finishing high school, the boy who had struggled to get through college, were all at loose ends. There was no organization except the Army that had the tents and other supplies essential for a setup of this kind, which was why part of the program was promptly put under its jurisdiction.

Franklin realized that the boys should be given some other kind of education as well, but it had to be subordinate to the day's labor required of them. The Civilian Conservation Corps had a triple value: it gave the boys a chance to see different parts of their own country, and to learn to do a good day's work in the open, which benefited them physically; also it gave them a cash income, part of which went home to their families. This helped the morale both of the boys themselves and of the people at home. The idea was his own contribution to the vast scheme of relief rehabilitation planning.

This was followed on June 16 by the National Recovery Act, with General Hugh Johnson in charge. The basic importance of the NRA was that it made it easier for the industrialist who wanted to do the right thing. The chiseler and the man who was willing to profit by beating down his labor could no longer compete unfairly with the man who wanted to earn a decent profit but to treat his employees fairly. The NRA was declared unconstitutional almost two years later. I thought this was unfortunate, for it seemed a simple way to keep bad employers doing what was right.

The Public Works Administration, which came into being on the same day, made it possible for the government to plan and undertake public works during this period of depression. It helped to take up the slack of unemployment by lending money to the states for projects that they could not finance by themselves.

Five months later, in November, 1933, the Civil Works Administration was set up and in time put four million unemployed to work.

In my travels around the country I saw many things built both by PWA and by CWA. I also saw the results of the work done by CCC. The achievements of these agencies began to dot city and rural areas alike. Soil conservation and forestry work went forward, recreation areas were built, and innumerable bridges, schools, hospitals and sanitation projects were constructed—lasting monuments to the good work done under these agencies. It is true they cost the people of the country vast sums of money, but they did a collective good and left tangible results which are evident today. They pulled the country out of the depression and made it possible for us to fight the greatest and most expensive war in our history.

Perhaps the most far-reaching project was the Tennessee Valley Authority. That was Senator George Norris' greatest dream and no one who witnessed the development of the Authority will ever forget the fight he put up for something that many people ridiculed. The development had been begun during World War I, but at the end of that war most of the work was stopped. Nothing further was done until my husband, who understood Senator Norris' vision, supplied the impetus at a time when it could accomplish the maximum results for the country. With the demands of a possible war in mind, Franklin insisted on pushing work on the TVA as rapidly as possible. He believed even then that under certain circumstances war might come soon, and he knew if that happened we would need everything the TVA could make available.

In the campaign of 1932 my husband and I had gone through some of the TVA area, and he had been deeply impressed by the crowds at the stations. They were so poor; their houses were unpainted, their cars were dilapidated, and many grownups as well as children were without shoes or adequate garments. Scarcely eight years later, after the housing and educational and agricultural experiments had had time to take effect, I went through the same area, and a more prosperous region would have been hard to find. I have always wished that those who oppose authorities to create similar benefits in the valleys of other great rivers could have seen the contrast as I saw it. I realize that such changes must come gradually, but I hate to see nothing done. I wish, as my husband always wished, that year by year we might be making a start on the Missouri River and the headwaters of the Mississippi. Such experiments, changing for the better the life of the people, would be a mighty bulwark against attacks on our democracy.

The CCC Changed My Life

Stanley Watson

The Civilian Conservation Corps (CCC) was one of Roosevelt's most successful New Deal agencies. It offered unemployed young men a chance to be productive by working outdoors. Over two and a half million young men were taken off the streets and put to work building roads, bridges, and dams, and reforesting. They were even paid $30 a month—most of which was made to go home to the parents. The author of the following article, Stanley Watson, describes his life hoboing around the country and how the educational opportunities the CCC offered changed his life. He later attended Washington State University and wrote a book about his experiences during the Depression.

Early in the winter of 1933 a ragged, shabby youth might have been seen trudging Westward upon the national highway bearing the number thirty. That youth was the writer of this article.

Out of work, discouraged, forsaken by those whom I thought to be my friends, and worst of all without a home or shelter to which to turn, I gathered my few belongings together and turned tramp. This was December 1933. Not knowing where I was going, I turned Westward, trudging disconsolately along the highway through a damp, cold snowstorm. Depending on passing motorists for rides, I progressed rapidly until I neared the great plains area. I was be-

Excerpted from *The Spirit of the Civilian Conservation Corps* (New York: Longmans, Green, and Co., 1937) by Stanley Watson.

coming sick and weak; the few dollars that I had had were gone; I was tired and hungry for the first time in my life.

Too Proud to Beg

Too proud to beg for my food, I continued on to North Platte, Nebraska, where cold weather forced me to ask humbly for shelter. I was provided with this in the way of a canvas cot at the city hall, but no feather bed or beauty rest mattress in the most expensive of hotels would have felt better to me than that strip of canvas stretched between two laths.

Morning dawned clear but exceedingly cold; the thermometer registered thirty-eight degrees below zero. My vanity would not allow me to ask for food after having been lodged for the night; so, weak from hunger, I resumed my journey Westward, with Cheyenne, Wyoming as my goal for night. The day grew steadily colder; the pangs of hunger gnawed upon my weakened body; but still I trudged onward, determined to reach my goal. Dusk and then darkness found me still short of my destination. At last I could see the lights of the city from a distance. My strength was failing rapidly; I tried to hurry but to no avail; I could no longer force myself to do the things against which nature rebelled.

At noon the next day I was gently awakened by a beautiful, dark-haired nurse and an army physician who wanted to know if I didn't care to have some beef broth or hot milk toast. I would rather have slept than eaten, but the doctor seemed to think I had slept long enough for the time being and insisted that I drink some broth. When I had finished, I asked him where I was and how I happened to be there. I was in the Station Hospital at Fort Warren, Wyoming. I had been picked up on the road outside of Cheyenne, overcome by lack of nourishment and over-exposure in the bitter cold. For two weeks I was confined to my bed and another week was spent regaining my strength before I was allowed again to take to the road.

When I left Cheyenne, I rode for the first time in a box car. My experience of the past few weeks had taught me a lesson. My pride vanished; I begged for my food and when

I could not get it, I stole from my fellow unfortunates just as they did. A week or ten days later, I was in Seattle where I stopped at the home of relatives to clean up before resuming my travels.

A Job in the Corps

When I had rested and refreshed myself, I started out bumming, begging my food and lodging, and pillaging when begging did not achieve the end to my satisfaction. I traveled in all of our forty-eight states, and I was rapidly becoming hardened to the coarser things of life. I went unshaven and dirty. I became lazy. Why should I work when I could eat three times a day without the outlay of a single copper or an ounce of energy? I became a master of sob-stories.

A Civilian Conservation Corps (CCC) team works on a reforesting project. The CCC offered young men $30 a month to work outdoors at various tasks.

After eighteen months of riding box cars, begging and robbing for my food, fighting, dodging policemen, and committing other forms of petty larceny, I arrived in the village of Woodridge, New York, where I called upon an aunt and uncle. They talked to me of an organization called the Civilian Conservation Corps in which I could earn $30 a month and my board and room; I was amazed. I had never heard of it but at their insistence I promised to enlist and try it for one enlistment period. At last I was to have a home and something constructive to do.

I was first stationed at Narrowsburg, New York, in the midst of the beautiful Catskill Mountains. There, on the twenty-third of July, 1934, I began a life of discipline and supervision. It was a strange new life, but being a good mixer and having had the discipline of the road, I soon took hold.

The work of Company 1245 was divided into four phases, namely, the building of fire lanes, clearing and burning of brush, blister rust control and army overhead work. It was in the latter group that it fell my lot to work. My first assignment was that of a "galley slave," kitchen scully or K.P., call it what you may; I peeled vegetables, washed dishes, and scrubbed floors until I almost did them in my sleep.

I did my daily work diligently and precisely, working always for the one thing that was uppermost in my mind—advancement. I was working with a tall, dark-complexioned fellow who afterward was to become my most devoted friend. Two cousins of mine also worked with me. I wanted to gain a cook's position; so I spent a good share of my spare time around the ranges helping the cooks whenever possible.

Weekends when there was no work, those of us who were close enough went home. I spent my weekends with my aunt and uncle. During these periods of relaxation from the routine work of camp we had parties, went to dances, and engaged in many other forms of recreational activity. All too soon came the exciting yet disappointing message that we were to move to California. The trip across the continent was, for me, very dull and uneventful as I had roamed around over this same country not six months before. We arrived in Virgilio, California on the twenty-eighth day of October and walked into a camp location that made us all wonder why we had ever left good old New York. We were resigned to our fate, however; and within a few weeks, with hard work, had our camp in a very presentable condition.

Educational Opportunities

As the months passed, new fellows came and the old went. With each coming and going, friendships were made and broken, new personalities appeared and new problems for those in charge. I recall one instance when a group of seven illiterates arrived in camp. The educational advisor, a young fellow just out of a well-known Midwestern school, threw up his hands in disgust. What could he do about it? He wasn't there to teach the alphabet; he had more important things to do. As a result these poor unfortunates went untutored. Those of us who had some education were given opportunity to advance ourselves. I studied sociology and sex hygiene—two very interesting and important subjects.

More recruits were coming into camp, and with each new group, the company's intelligence quotient dropped several points. The educational advisor (we had a new one) was very much disturbed but did little to remedy the fact. By January 1935 there were no less than fifteen illiterates in camp and had the educational record of the camp been published, it would probably read something like this: 7 per cent illiterate, 25 per cent with fourth-grade records, 40 per cent with eighth-grade diplomas, 30 per cent had entered high school but did not finish, and 3 per cent had high school diplomas. Not a very imposing tabulation for a group of 200, but nevertheless true.

March came and with it the end of an enlistment period. My dark-complexioned friend was going home; I tried to talk him into staying but he begged me to go home with him. Neither of us could see his way clear to accommodate the other. With our tears of parting mingled with those of others, we split the trail. March was an eventful month for me. I lost the only real pal and friend I had in camp; I achieved my ambition and was rated a first cook, but best of all, the camp got an educational advisor with plenty of vim, vigor, and vitality. He stamped so strong an impression on me that I shall never forget him. He was short, fat, very jovial, and extremely well educated.

He received his Bachelor of Science and Master of Science degrees from Washington State College; and above all he had an active interest in his work. He not only saw the deplorable situation in our camp but took steps to overcome them. He selected three of us who he knew had high school diplomas and made us his helpers. He then divided the group of illiterates equally among us and told us to get to work. We did and thought the work was interesting from a psychological standpoint, but it was slow and tedious. After six months of constant teaching, all of the fifteen fellows were reading and writing.

A class in Poultry Husbandry was organized which I attended with intense interest. The educational advisor took a real liking to me and it was through his ever-ready tutoring and constant insistence that a new ambition was born within me. I decided to further my education, to go on to college. I worked diligently and saved my pay checks. Soon after deciding to go to college, I gained another promotion; I was made mess steward. In this capacity I gained experience that was to stand me in good stead later.

Eager to Move On

Evenings I took advantage of the many educational advantages offered to the enrollees. I studied Psychology, Sociology, and Speech. Through the winter I worked with but one picture in my mind—that of a beautiful green campus with big brick buildings and of myself going to and from classes—a beautiful picture if only it could be realized.

Spring came and summer. With each passing day, I looked forward with renewed eagerness to the day when I should say "Adieu" to my friends and again carry a textbook under my arm. Knowing that I would have to work my way through, I made several applications for work and received many offers, two of which I answered and accepted. Both were for cooks. Thank Heaven I had applied myself in this line for the duration of my enlistment. The knowledge I had acquired in the planning and preparation of meals was now to be a benefit.

On September the ninth I arrived in Pullman, Washington, to begin my duties; on the eighteenth I was enrolled and registered as a member in full standing in the freshman class. At the present time I am doing on the average of twenty-five hours work a week and am carrying a full schedule of school work. While I am not an outstanding student, I am managing to keep afloat and in pace with the average students of my class. My dreams have been realized, thanks to an educational advisor and the lessons learned in the CCC.

Chronology

1928
Herbert Clark Hoover is elected president of the United States.

1929
The stock market crashes in October, sending millions of investors into bankruptcy.

1930
The Hawley-Smoot Tariff Act is passed, raising import tariffs as high as 50 percent; nations raise their own tariffs for American goods and worsen the effects of the Great Depression for all involved.

1931
Hostilities begin between Japan and China; Hoover creates the Reconstruction Finance Corporation to help keep U.S. banks, railroads, and insurance companies from failing.

1932
Veterans of the First World War who call themselves the Bonus Expeditionary Force travel to Washington to collect money promised to them by Congress; Franklin Delano Roosevelt is elected president of the United States.

1933
Adolf Hitler becomes chancellor of Germany; Roosevelt declares a four-day bank holiday to ease panic and determine which banks are solvent enough to reopen; FDR uses the radio to broadcast the first Fireside Chat to the country; the New Deal begins with the approval of fifteen acts, including the creation of the Civilian Conservation Corps, the

Agricultural Adjustment Act, and the National Recovery Administration; Prohibition is repealed.

1934

The Securities and Exchange Act, which regulates Wall Street trading, is passed.

1935

The Social Security Act, providing pensions for old-age retirement and unemployment compensation is signed; the Works Progress Administration is formed to create work for artists, musicians, writers, and actors; Italy invades Ethiopia.

1936

Roosevelt is reelected president; the Olympics open in Berlin.

1937

The "Roosevelt" Recession of 1937–1938 begins; unemployment rises to 20 percent.

1938

Germany occupies the Sudetenland; the Fair Labor Standards Act is passed, establishing a forty-hour workweek and the nation's first minimum wage.

1939

Germany invades Czechoslovakia and Poland; Britain and France in turn declare war on Germany, beginning the Second World War; John Steinbeck's *The Grapes of Wrath* is published; orders for war materials from Europe flood into the United States, ending the Great Depression of the 1930s.

For Further Research

Frederick Lewis Allen, *Since Yesterday*. New York: Bantam Books, 1940.

Benjamin Appel, *The People Talk*. New York: E.P. Dutton, 1940.

Nathan Asch, *The Road*. New York: W.W. Norton, 1937.

Ann Banks, *First-Person America*. New York: Alfred A. Knopf, 1980.

Paul Bonnifield, *The Dust Bowl: Men, Dirt, and Depression*. Albuquerque: University of New Mexico Press, 1979.

James Seay Brown Jr., ed., *Up Before Daylight: Life Histories from the Alabama Writers' Project, 1938–1939*. Tuscaloosa: University of Alabama Press, 1982.

Roger A. Bruns, *Knights of the Road: A Hobo History*. New York: Methuen Books, 1980.

Russell D. Buhite and David W. Levy, eds., *FDR's Fireside Chats*. New York: Penguin Books, 1992.

Andrew Carroll, ed., *Letters of a Nation: A Collection of Extraordinary American Letters*. New York: Kodansha America, 1997.

Don Congdon, *The 30's: A Time to Remember*. New York: Simon and Schuster, 1962.

W.T. Couch, ed., *These Are Our Lives: As Told by the People and Written by Members of the Federal Writers' Project of the Works Progress Administration in North Carolina, Tennessee, Georgia*. New York: W.W. Norton, 1975.

Bernard Edelman, *The Story of the Twentieth Century by the Americans Who Lived It*. New York: Farrar, Straus, and Giroux, 1999.

Jacqueline Farrell, *The Great Depression*. San Diego: Lucent Books, 1996.

Frank Freidel, ed., *The New Deal and the American People.* Englewood Cliffs, NJ: Prentice Hall, 1964.

Harvey Green, *The Uncertainty of Everyday Life: 1915–1945.* New York: HarperPerennial, 1993.

Harlan Miners Speak: Report on Terrorism in the Kentucky Coal Fields Prepared by Members of the National Committee for the Defense of Political Prisoners. New York: Da Capo Press, 1970.

Robert J. Hastings, *A Nickel's Worth of Skim Milk: A Boy's View of the Great Depression.* Carbondale: Southern Illinois University Press, 1972.

June Havoc, *Early Havoc.* New York: Simon and Schuster, 1959.

Anna Arnold Hedgeman, *The Trumpet Sounds: A Memoir of Negro Leadership.* New York: Holt, Rinehart, and Winston, 1964.

Russ Hofvendahl, *A Land So Fair and Bright: A True Story of a Young Man's Adventures Across Depression America.* New York: Sheridan House, 1991.

G.C. Jones, *Growing Up Hard in Harlan County.* Lexington: University Press of Kentucky, 1985.

Matthew Josephson, *The Money Lords.* New York: Weybright and Talley, 1972.

Ann Marie Low, *Dust Bowl Diary.* Lincoln: University of Nebraska Press, 1984.

Frank Marquart, *An Auto Worker's Journal: The UAW from Crusade to One-Party Union.* Philadelphia: Pennsylvania State University Press, 1975.

Robert McElvaine, *Down and Out in the Great Depression: Letters from the "Forgotten Man."* Chapel Hill: University of North Carolina Press, 1983.

Milton Meltzer, *Brother Can You Spare a Dime?* New York: Alfred A. Knopf, 1969.

Thomas Minehan, *Boy and Girl Tramps of America.* New York: Grosset & Dunlap, 1934.

Dennis Nishi, *Life During the Great Depression.* San Diego: Lucent Books, 1998.

Gordon Parks, *A Choice of Weapons.* New York: Harper & Row, 1966.

Ben L. Reitman, *Sister of the Road: An Autobiography of Box-Car Bertha*, as Told to Dr. Ben L. Reitman. New York: Macaulay, 1937.

Eleanor Roosevelt, *The Autobiography of Eleanor Roosevelt.* New York: Harper & Brothers, 1937.

Gilbert Seldes, *The Years of the Locust: America, 1929–1932.* Boston: Little, Brown, 1933.

Eric Sevareid, *Not So Wild a Dream.* New York: Alfred A. Knopf, 1946.

Rita James Simon, ed., *As We Saw the Thirties: Essays on Social and Political Movements of a Decade.* Urbana: University of Illinois Press, 1967.

Jerry Stanley, *Children of the Dustbowl: The True Story of the School at Weedpatch Camp.* New York: Crown Books, 1993.

John Steinbeck, *The Grapes of Wrath.* New York: Alfred A. Knopf, 1993.

Bernard Sternsher and Judith Sealander, eds., *Women of Valor: The Struggle Against the Great Depression as Told in Their Own Life Stories.* Chicago: Ivan R. Dee, 1990.

Harvey Swados, ed., *The American Writer and the Great Depression.* New York: Bobbs Merrill, 1966.

Studs Terkel, *Hard Times.* New York: Pantheon Books, 1970.

Tome E. Terrill and Jerrold Hirsch, eds., *Such as Us: Southern Voices of the Thirties.* Chapel Hill: University of North Carolina Press, 1978.

Tom Tiede, *American Tapestry: Eyewitness Accounts of the Twentieth Century.* New York: Pharos Books, 1988.

Rexford G. Tugwell, *Roosevelt's Revolution: The First Year: A Personal Perspective.* New York: Macmillan, 1977.

Errol Lincoln Uys, *Riding the Rails: Teenagers on the Move During the Great Depression*. New York: TV Books, 1999.

W.W. Waters, as told to William C. White, *The Whole Story of the Bonus Army*. New York: John Day, 1933.

T.H. Watkins, *The Great Depression: America in the 1930s*. Boston: Little, Brown, 1993.

———, *The Hungry Years: A Narrative History of the Great Depression in America*. New York: Henry Holt, 1999.

Jeane Westin, *Making Do: How Women Survived the '30s*. Chicago: Follett, 1976.

Index